Renaming the Earth

Camino del Sol
A Latina and Latino Literary Series

Renaming the Earth

PERSONAL ESSAYS

Ray Gonzalez

the university of arizona press   tucson

The University of Arizona Press
© 2008 Ray Gonzalez
All rights reserved

Library of Congress Cataloging-in-Publication Data appear
on the last printed page of this book.

Publication of this book is made possible in part by the
proceeds of a permanent endowment created with the assistance of a Challenge Grant from the National Endowment
for the Humanities, a federal agency.

Manufactured in the United States of America on acid-
free, archival-quality paper.

13   12   11   10   09   08   6   5   4   3   2   1

Contents

Part One

A Different Border

I want to stand on a different U.S.–Mexican border that accepts the fusion of English and Spanish that dominates El Paso. You can say it is bilingual or *caló* or Spanglish, whatever. On a different border, the language would be taught, made official, and accepted outside of the Southwest with its blend of Mexican and American cultures. This speech with its origins in two countries is spoken here all the time. Who cares if it is official or not? You don't have to teach it. Growing up in a border town like El Paso includes naturally picking up the bi-tongue and expressing it. I like that combination—bi-tongue. Two roots, two mouths, two ways of expressing how we live and how we survive in a region that has redefined what it means to live in the United States. Most El Pasoans don't realize that by living on the border they have created a unique America.

A different border would also mean a lower poverty rate, less crime, and the taming of a highly visible and dramatic racism—a separation to be tested further by the intrusion of National Guard troops and the plans to build a longer wall between the United States and Mexico. It would end the erosion of cultural traditions from native Mexico and reinforce traditions created by earlier generations of Mexican Americans, who had to change their way of life and adapt to living in the United States. Whenever I visit El Paso, I drive around the area and gaze at the slow destruction of the city's infrastructure, its monuments, its heritage, and watch as the new El Paso rises out of the desert, unable to decide if it is a version of twenty-first-century Mexico or an island of bilingual Americans with their own habits, beliefs, and ways of doing things. As I drive up and down Interstate 10, I can see the Rio Grande and the shacks of the *colonias* east of Juárez that dot the dusty hills by the river. I make my way through central El Paso, and those shacks reappear on city streets, on either side of alleys, and around empty lots that are the latest image of a place tearing down the old to keep up with the new. The *El Paso Times* runs regular stories on the plight of the economy and celebrates the fact that seven thousand more army troops are being sent to Fort Bliss in the next few years. The newspaper quotes businessmen who are pleased that more young people in uniform are arriving because they will spend more money in El Paso.

What does this have to do with a different border? Mexico's illegal immigration problem and the tightening of security along the border after September 11, 2001, will affect things, but they will never create an invulnerable border. Such a thing doesn't exist; it never has, and, despite the current mania against immigrants, it never will. El Paso is located in an isolated region of West Texas, and the area is known as one of the top drug-smuggling regions in the country. Younger generations of Mexican American kids on El Paso streets can't speak Spanish and don't know what the word *Chicano* means. El Paso means the loss of jobs, but also cheap labor where you can find it and where employers have to use that labor to survive and maybe profit. Cheap labor and profits go hand in hand, and new anti-immigration legislation in these repressive times will not change anything. Another problem is a weak tourist trade because city officials have lagged behind other cities in creating attractive museums or places where people can go when they don't want to cross the international bridge and wind up in Juárez. The fear of going to Juárez because of the hundreds of young women who have been mysteriously murdered there permeates the area. El Paso is a city that has always had a confidence problem, an image problem, a passive-aggressive resistance to both change and finding ways to integrate its beauty and history into that change. I can make this grand conclusion because I am a native El Pasoan and can never forget its history in the midst of political forces that constantly tear at the city's ancient foundations.

The military has come back to life with the war in Iraq and the patriotic fever of thousands of families in El Paso. I go to malls and movie theaters here and spot young men and women in fatigues everywhere. One of the latest to be wounded in Iraq is shown on local television. A nineteen-year-old soldier named Ben Gonzalez is carried off a hospital plane as his family waits for him. He is nineteen years old, and his future as a normal person is in doubt as he faces a long recovery period and rehabilitation. Ben Gonzalez. No relation, though the television pictures also remind me of the fact that Iraq has already hit home on my mother's side of the family. Tony Mena, my nineteen-year-old nephew and the youngest of three sons, is beginning his second tour of duty in that war-torn country. The different border in 2006 is one where the military is dominant in the news, in the economy, and in the daily life of El Paso.

Does a different border mean that the violent history of the conquest of the Americas, the settling of the West, the genocide of native people, and the racism arising from a dual way of life along an international boundary line have come full circle because the region is proud to highlight its contribution to American imperialism—a strong military presence that is extending the long history of Fort Bliss's impact on El Paso? The area can't solve its illegal immigration problem, its lack of jobs, and its high poverty rate, but it can certainly support the troops and depend on them to show people there is one aspect of living on the border that the entire nation can accept.

The border is becoming different when El Paso looks like an armed camp, not in the traditional sense of many Texans' owning guns or being able to carry them because of laws allowing concealed handguns, and not even in the almost stereotyped sense of drug dealers, cheap pot, and drug cartels fighting it out across the river in Juárez. Because of George W. Bush, El Paso resembles an armed camp because there are military personnel all over the city, spilling over from Fort Bliss and dumping millions of dollars on the local, desperate economy. I have stated this before, but repeat again because I have not seen such an intense patriotic fever as the one I find in El Paso in the summer of 2004. American flags everywhere, along with bumper stickers and signs supporting the war in Iraq. Young people love the patriotism, and I don't mean the nineteen- and twenty-year-olds who appear all over town in their fatigues. I mean local citizens and members of military families whose time under the Southwest sun includes waving the flag, supporting George Bush, and proclaiming that their sons, husbands, wives, and daughters are doing their duty so "America can be safer." El Paso has always been a conservative town, and, again, Fort Bliss has a long tradition in the area, but this latest rallying around the war is stunning. Sure, a large military population is going to reflect its beliefs, but, as a native of the area, I feel the militaristic drama is somehow out of place here. Many natives and experts on El Paso will laugh at me and ask, "What did you expect? This is Texas, and this is surely a military town." The answer is not that simple, though, because El Paso, situated on the tip of West Texas, had developed its own version of a New Mexico Native American posture that kept the city years behind the national times and reinforced the notion that El Pasoans were sleepy, passive, politically naive people. In other words, El Paso had the reputation of being one of the conquered, not the one doing the conquering. Today's different border has changed that. The Stars and

Stripes have woken El Paso and put a pair of cojones on it. One question to explore is, What eventually will become one of the key factors in the new border dynamics—the eternal clash between Mexicans, Anglos, and Mexican Americans, or the rise of the new military metropolis that, to me, is a major contradiction of the old El Paso and its vanished way of life?

I fly into El Paso on the hottest day the region has had—107 degrees—and enter the furnace of the desert as if I had never lived here. I sit next to a couple of young people returning to Fort Bliss—a young woman in the military, twenty-three years old, who tells the man sitting next to her that she would rather be stationed in Kuwait and Iraq, from which she is returning, than cross the border into Juárez. The forty-year-old black man agrees and says that Juárez is more dangerous than the Middle East. I am stunned to hear this and can't believe two people in the army would rather face the dangers of the war than life on the U.S.–Mexican border. The girl, a mechanic whose unit came under attack during the first stages of the invasion of Baghdad a few years ago, laughs and says, "Yeah, give me the terrorists over there any day. That's not as hard to take as all the dead girls they keep finding in Juárez." They continue talking about their military lives throughout the flight from Houston to El Paso. She had started the conversation by asking the stranger where he was stationed. When he told her he worked for the government and didn't reveal the line of work, she said, "I thought only military fly into El Paso these days." I try not to listen to their conversation after that, but the crowded flight has us sitting side by side. I keep reading my book, but pay attention to one final statement the girl makes before we glide in for a rough landing in El Paso. "Yeah, we train harder and we fight harder because our commander in chief made a mistake." We arrive.

There are metal bars on the windows of houses in the neighborhood where I grew up, though El Paso has been declared one of the safest cities in the United States, apparently because of a low crime rate. My mother's house does not have any bars, and she has refused over the decades to install any as a deterrent against crime, but it is stunning to see house after house covered with bars, all on the streets where I grew up as a boy. There was no such thing as reinforcing your home against theft and burglary in the 1950s and 1960s. It wasn't an issue. Now my old neighborhood has been transformed by the high number of houses whose owners have chosen to bar their windows. What has changed in thirty-five years? As someone who grew up in the area, I have always known that illegal immigrants crossed to work on this side of the border, but no one ever cited an increase in crime because of their presence or their need to find work in El Paso. Many people, including my family who live here, say the people are putting bars on their windows because the Mexicans are out of control and breaking into homes and because the crime rate has soared. If this is true, why wasn't the crime rate so explosive decades ago? Why didn't people bar their windows back then? Why did my neighborhood feel so safe when I was growing up? Did that sense of peace come from being a naive boy, or were people from Mexico more peaceful back then? What has made them so aggressive and criminal now? Plus, am I making conclusions bordering on stereotypes? Have people barred their windows to keep illegal Mexicans out because illegal Mexicans are the only ones breaking into houses? Of course not, but the barring of windows also says a great deal about the criminal population on the border these days.

My favorite movie theater in El Paso is gone. It was located two miles from my mother's house in a fairly new strip mall. I went to dozens of movies there over the past twenty years of visiting my family. It was always convenient to go to a movie there during my regular visits. On this latest trip, I drive by to see what is showing and find that the theater has been turned into several small shops. No more movies there, my cool sanctuary in the desert erased as if that cocoon of solitude was too good to be true. There are other multiplex theaters nearby, with the closest one in the giant mall, but watching movies in the desert will never be the same.

I eat my first great Mexican food in a restaurant by the oldest cemetery in El Paso. The L & R Café has a gordita special for lunch, a rare item on most Mexican menus, so I do not hesitate. I park my car along a row of vehicles that have pulled against one of the stone walls of the cemetery. I am always looking for Mexican restaurants I have not tried in El Paso and have found them in unusual corners of the city, but have never eaten right next to the historical burial ground. My great-grandmother, Josefina, is buried there. So is John Wesley Hardin, the infamous Texas outlaw who was gunned down in a saloon in El Paso in the late 1880s. His grave was lost for most of the twentieth century, but was rediscovered several decades ago. As I get out of my car and start to cross the street toward the busy L & R, I realize Hardin's resting place is on the other side of the wall where hungry customers park to eat tacos, burritos, and hot green chili. I turn and stare at the high wall to make sure I am correct. Yes, this is the far southwestern corner of Concordia, and the outlaw lies right over there, beyond that Honda Accord and the fancy Ford pickup truck. Fine Mexican food right next to the cemetery. I go inside, eat one of the best meals I have had in several years, and think about the thousands of marked and unmarked graves a few yards from where I sit, the packed café and bar loud and busy. The lunch crowd grows as I try to come up with some connection between Mexican food, dead people, and acres of gravestones and markers that have accepted the dead for the past 150 years.

In my ramblings, I also stumble upon Steak Pedo, a subway sandwich business in the food court of the Sunland Park Mall. I go to the mall to look for summer shorts and pass by the busy food court. There is a huge line of people at Steak Pedo. I usually wouldn't notice the long row of awful fast-food restaurants, but Steak Pedo catches my eye because *pedo* is the Spanish word for "fart." The name of the place is Steak Pedo, and signs everywhere announce "Steak Pedo" with a colorful photo of a huge steak sandwich under the name.

Downtown El Paso contains block after block of used clothing stores and pawnshops, many of them catering to Mexicans from Juárez who cross the border legally to shop. One of the largest pawnshops is marked by a huge plaster statue of Elvis in a white jumpsuit, playing a guitar. On either side of the life-size Elvis are the Blues Brothers, John Belushi and Dan Ackroyd, dressed in their Chicago finest—dark suits, shades, and hats—Belushi clutching a huge microphone in his pink hands. Right next door is Shooter's Supply, a scary-looking gun and ammunition store, though the way the storefront is decorated makes it look like a cross between a year-round haunted house and a military fortress. The windows display an arsenal of every type of gun, rifle, knife, and other weapons, along with manikins in camouflage outfits. On first seeing the place, I think about going inside, but I never get the nerve to enter.

I saw a different border when I realized I no longer had to search for home. Home was El Paso. It always had been, and the years of wanting it to be something else were gone. The border town has changed with its larger population, its destruction of old buildings, and the rooting of a twenty-first-century Latino culture that is a hybrid nation of Mexican nationals who want a life in the United States and Mexican Americans who want to be accepted as the majority and see themselves as "Americans," without the word *Mexican* in front of the label. Growing up in El Paso made it difficult for me to see this kind of culture develop over the decades. Border life has transformed the segregated little town of my childhood into a metropolis of fast Latino zip codes. I will say it again—fast Latino zip codes. In other words—fast cars, low- to medium-paying jobs, strip malls, fancy restaurants, endless rows of new apartment complexes all looking the same, a macho and rather conservative lifestyle, the bilingual tongue of *"carros,* tenees, TV, popcorn," and other mutations of English and Spanish. The Latino zip code means El Paso is populated by a younger, well-educated generation of Latinos, many of them born and raised in other parts of the country. They have somehow wound up in El Paso for high-tech jobs and industry, the civilian sector supporting Fort Bliss and its large military population. Many of them are also here for unknown reasons, both legal and illegal. The evolving border allows the Latino zip code occupant to play out a daily routine of cell phone calls inside new Hondas and Toyotas screaming down Interstate 10 on the way to work or to happy hour or for a quick lunch with friends at the latest trendy Mexican restaurant. This scene sounds cynical and very American, but it is far removed from the border that shaped the ancient, quiet, small town of the old El Paso I used to know.

The different border has done away with Chicano pride from the 1960s and 1970s, has torn down old Catholic churches from a pre–World War II landscape, and has stretched the city limits beyond the horizon. El Paso cannot be tied down to old border ways any longer because generations of illegal immigration, drug dealing, cheap labor, segregation, only half-successful integration, the rise and fall of thousands of small businesses, and a poor public-education system jockey for position with the Latino zip code—again, a world where the cell phone, the quick beer, the rented apartment, and the low-paying job (compared to the rest of the United States, that is, though great for El Paso) say you can be young and happy on the border. You can play and work and sleep and fuck and do drugs or drink and go to the latest movie in the new stadium-seating theater or marvel at the very first Best Buy electronics store to open in town. The Latino zip code dweller could care less about "illegal aliens," U.S. Border Patrol abuses, the destruction of the environment at the hands of North American Free Trade Agreement (NAFTA) overlords, and the fact that Texas ranks next to last in every quality-of-life survey (New Mexico is fiftieth). Believe it or not, the Latino zip code dweller often votes Republican and has no sense of history when it comes to the desert Southwest. It is a different border because the need to assimilate, or become "American," has called for the extermination of the old boundaries that kept El Paso on its desert island.

In my most recent book on El Paso, I wrote about various unusual museums in the region. Taking a look at museums is one of the best and most compact ways to illustrate heritage tourism—the art of rewriting history to draw tourist dollars. An editorial in the *El Paso Times*, appearing several years after my book, catches my attention. Written by Enrique N. Medrano, a member of the El Paso County Historical Society, the guest column calls for the city to invest millions of dollars in new museums that will help revitalize downtown. Medrano acknowledges that the city is already building its history museum downtown, but he wants to add the Old El Paso Museum at the corner of El Paso and San Antonio Streets. He likes this location because John Wesley Hardin had a law office upstairs. Of course, this eternal resident of Concordia cemetery is better known as an outlaw, but Medrano claims that the historic corner building will draw thousands of people. The Old El Paso Museum would showcase El Paso's outlaws, he writes. According to Medrano, tourists from all over the world would come see where Hardin had his law office. Why would people from all over the world flock to the law office of an Old West outlaw? Does Medrano really believe that would be a draw when even most El Pasoans today have no idea who John Wesley Hardin is?

The idea that really stands out in Medrano's article is the establishment of the Museum of the Mexican Revolution. El Paso and Juárez were key sites for the plotting of the rebellion and include locations of several battles. Pancho Villa had several homes in El Paso. The problem with Medrano's idea is that it would cause a stir on both sides of the border. Many Mexicans still hate Pancho Villa, and many Americans don't like him and love to stereotype him as the greatest Mexican bandit. A few years ago another member of the Historical Society suggested that El Paso erect statues of famous people who contributed to its wild history. Pancho Villa was on the list of figures, but the idea was shot down instantly by city officials and several local citizens who still see Villa as the bad guy. Medrano thinks small by saying that thousands of tourists would flock to Hardin's law office. He more expansively claims that "hundreds of thousands" of tourists would come see the Caples Building at Mesa and San Antonio Streets, the site used by a revolutionary junta in the early planning of the revolt. Medrano says the building would be the ideal spot for a revolution museum. Topping Medrano's dream of a historical mecca in El Paso is his suggestion of a 1966 Miner Men's Basketball Championship Museum. The University of Texas at El Paso (UTEP) basketball team is legendary for being the first college team to win a national title with five black players as starters. Their famous victory over the University of Kentucky was made into a 2004 film that drew national attention to El Paso, but has faded into the wilderness of mediocre sports movies. Medrano claims that hundreds of thousands of new tourists will make their way to El Paso to visit these amazing museums. I make a copy of his article at the El Paso Public Library and realize that one of the thickest files I have on my hometown contains column after newspaper column written by local historians and promoters of El Paso's past, whose cries for a wise revitalization of the city, based on highlighting its past, go unheard year after year.

Wandering through Sunland Park Mall near my mother's house, I go into a Suncoast media store, a national chain that sells DVDs. I never know what I will find in one and have come across hard-to-find old movies and rock music concert discs in Suncoasts from the Twin Cities area. I don't expect much from the Sunland Park one, but am surprised and delighted to come across a copy of John Carpenter's *Dark Star*, an obscure 1974 science-fiction film whose little known re-release on DVD is making some fanatics of Carpenter's weird films start to claim that *Dark Star* will become a cult classic. I have never seen it, but have read several reviews of the disc version. It is about a spaceship that has been hurtling through space for twenty years. Its crew is made up of hippie astronauts whose long hair and beards, rock music, drugs, and wacko antics are necessary to survive the trip. It is a "dark" comedy, Carpenter's take on 1960s culture and the U.S. obsession with outer space following the NASA moon walks late in that decade. The first DVD I ever bought for my strange film collection was Carpenter's remake of the old 1950s classic *The Thing*, and I have been interested in some of his other work, though I have passed on several of his mediocre vampire films. I had searched in the Twin Cities for a copy of *Dark Star*, had pondered ordering it through Amazon.com, but here it is in El Paso—one copy originally priced at $25 on sale for only $9.99. I grab it, and in my glee at the counter I tell the clerk that the DVD is hard to find. He looks at me suspiciously when the cash register drops the full price down to the great sales price and stares at the disc.

I put the disc into the media program on the laptop I travel with and can see right away why Carpenter fanatics might be giddy over this hilarious film. Of course, the underlying and serious hit on our culture of the 1960s is the fact that the spaceship, the *Dark Star*, carries nuclear bombs that can destroy "unstable" planets. Each bomb has a number and its own voice, and each talks back to the astronauts. A rogue bomb eventually disobeys computer orders from the ship, disengages from the bomb bay, and hangs below *Dark Star*, ready to blow its unstable crew into darkness. Funny, but I can't follow the story or laugh yet because the opening scene and credits startle me when one of the hippie astronauts presses a button and a song called "Benson, Arizona" starts to play. It is an odd country-western tune I have never heard before.

I can't believe it because Benson, Arizona, is my mother's birthplace! The old railroad town lies east of Tucson and will probably soon be swallowed up by that city's spreading population, but my grandfather's family lived there in the 1920s and 1930s when he was a crew foreman on the railroad. Benson, Arizona. What was John Carpenter doing putting a song called "Benson, Arizona" into a crazy film about spaced-out astronauts? My mother's hometown is being sung about in this bizarre sci-fi joke. Is this the reason I have been searching for a copy? The singer, whoever he is, does a cheap imitation of Johnny Cash and sings, "How I miss the desert skies. My body flies the galaxies. Benson, Arizona, blows the wind through your hair. My heart longs to be there. Benson, Arizona, the same stars in the sky. They seem kinder when we watch them, you and I."

I have wanted to write about the heat in El Paso and its powerful furnace atmosphere during the summer. Living in Minnesota with its cool, though often humid summers, I miss the hot intensity of the desert in July. The border would be different if it truly had four seasons, but it doesn't. Climate is one of the reasons why many people retire in this area. Despite the scorching temperatures during the summer, the attraction to this area could be an extension of the Southwest's reputation as the place where perfect weather (and to many people the heat is perfect) can keep you going, keep you awake and alive. In the 1870s and 1880s, thousands of people from all over the country were sent by their doctors to New Mexico for "climate therapy." They came to the desert to cure their tuberculosis. In the late nineteenth century, doctors claimed that pulmonary tuberculosis was the number one health problem of an industrial society. By 1920, there were forty sanatoriums, or "sans," in New Mexico. One of the largest and most popular was the Holy Ghost Sanatorium in Deming, though you could check into one in Las Cruces and Santa Fe or in more remote towns like Lincoln and Carlsbad. Treatments used previously, such as bleeding the ill person two or three times a week, did not work, so doctors decided good air would do the trick. Climate therapy involved spending a long amount of time breathing in New Mexico. Doctors assured their seriously ill patients that the high altitude of the desert had purer air and lower air pressure that would heal their sick lungs. Plus, the heat and the strong sun were there to back up the purity of the New Mexico environment. New Mexico became a health seeker's haven and attracted hundreds of doctors. Some historians claim the care and treatment of tuberculosis was an essential factor in the economic development of New Mexico in the late nineteenth century. The Great Depression of the 1930s brought all that to an end, however. No more sans were opened, and many closed after World War II. The evolution of medical science led to other treatments for tuberculosis, and doctors concluded that rest, good food, high altitude, and the pure air of New Mexico did not contribute to curing TB.

The regenerated border keeps bringing me back to the dominant role of Mexican food. Mexican culinary delights have an immense power that continues to influence and shape border culture. By "shape," I do not mean making it overweight, though Mexican food goes heavy in that direction. Mexican food can be used to measure how racist stereotypes (bean and tortilla eaters, Frito Bandidos) have become rooted among its consumers. The commercialization and creation of Mex-slop (Taco Bell) and the fact Mexican food is found in every state in the United States say that its staples are everywhere, cooked in a thousand different ways that are far removed from its authentic, delicious origins. If you grew up in El Paso, you can rightly claim it makes the best Mexican food in the United States. If you are new to the border, your taste buds can be numbed by new heights of jalapeño strength or the soft delicacy of homemade tortillas. If you live in other parts of the United States and have known real Mexican food, you can pretend that the Mexican restaurant in St. Paul, Minnesota, comes close. In the end, the new border is the fresh-smelling border where its people put an incredible energy into the cooking, selling, and eating of Mexican food. The result is that this food has a power unique in the area and is a magnetic force beyond the mouth and stomach, a force that most El Pasoans depend on daily to get by.

Yet the fluid border and its food face great challenges. Promoters of Mexico's traditional fast foods are fighting McDonalds, Burger King, Pizza Hut, KFC, and other foreign chains that are competing with sales of tortillas, tacos, and *tortas*. The Associated Press reports on Mexico's first Torta Festival in Mexico City. They hope to promote the overstuffed sandwich of bread, beans, and cheese and to offset the fact that Mexicans are eating more American hamburgers, fried chicken, and pizza these days instead of their traditional on-the-run staples of tacos and quesadillas. The news report quotes Francisco Juárez, head of the Mexican National Restaurant Chamber's Mexico City chapter, as saying, "The torta is not in danger of extinction, but its sales have declined by 50 percent over the last decade because of the competition from pizza and hamburgers." Between 1998 and 2004, tortilla consumption fell by 25 percent, from an average 308 pounds per person per year to 228 pounds, according to the National Corn Processors Chamber. After reading these numbers, I wonder how anyone could measure how many tortillas or pounds of tortilla a person ate in one year? Did they do a survey or ask? Who monitored this study? The point is not to question the data, but to give way to the magnitude of tortilla consumption and the reality that Mexican food's once invisible hold on people is weakening. This trend fits right into a new border landscape where perhaps too many false and awful mutations of authentic Mexican food have destroyed people's tastes and sent them elsewhere. The survey was conducted in interior Mexico, but tastes and trends immigrate, legally or illegally, toward the north, where larger and fatter consumers of Mexican food wipe their lips with their napkins and serve themselves a second or third helping.

It may not be very nice to criticize people's food habits considering that I love Mexican food and gorge on it whenever I visit El Paso, but my time in the great restaurants that I try for the first time is ruined a bit when I read the incredible headline in the *El Paso Times*, "Agents Strive to Keep Immigrants Nourished." In a region with a long history of abuse of illegal immigrants, it is hard to believe that Border Patrol agents are actually feeding good Mexican food to individuals they capture every day. The U.S. government usually issues turkey sandwiches with potato chips and apple juice to hungry illegal immigrants caught by the Border Patrol. The policy is that if an immigrant has not eaten in more than four hours, he or she must be fed. Most of them get granola bars, boxed juices, and microwaved frozen burritos kept at the Paso del Norte Bridge facility. The supplies also include baby bottles, formula, and diapers. The annual budget for these items is $50,000 in El Paso. Remote Border Patrol stations make their own arrangements. In changing times, agents are making runs to many restaurants and fast-food joints to feed men, women, and children in detention cells because the chains are best equipped to handle large orders. In Fabens, Texas, the "illegals" love McDonalds. In Deming, New Mexico, they order frozen meals from Amigos Mexican Food. In Carlsbad, they go to Wendy's and Taco Bell, but a large number of agents there order at Lucy's Mexican Restaurant, a local landmark. OK. More business is pumped into the economy by Border Patrol agents' walking up and down rows of jail cells taking orders. Forty orders per week at Lucy's may influence the way the owner, Lucy Yañez, might feel about immigration laws and tighter borders. Anti-immigration activists, mostly racist and right-wing, constantly scream for a harder crackdown. Do that, and Lucy is out forty orders per week.

My brother-in law Willie Mena used to work in an immigrant detention center when he was in his early twenties. Thirty years ago undocumented immigrants who were caught and incarcerated rarely got fed. One night during his shift, a Willie who was very green at his new job found himself being asked for food by a crowd of young Mexican boys. "Algo pa' comer, Meester," they kept shouting at him from behind bars. In the first few days of working at the center, Willie noticed an old Mexican woman with long white hair who was the cook in the center. He wasn't sure if she cooked for the Border Patrol agents or if she did feed some of the captured Mexicans. He noticed that she did not like the illegal immigrants and was hostile to them. The night of the mass begging for food was too much for Willie, and he gave in, stormed into the center's kitchen, dug through several refrigerators, and found a huge baloney sausage. With echoes of "Dame de comer, Meester" at his back, Willie quickly sliced the baloney and made sandwiches. This was a major mistake because the next day when the old woman found out what he had done, she threw a fit, tore into him, and kept repeating, "Son de halla! Son de halla!" She kept screaming at him that they were from "over there, over there"—Mexico. Thirty years ago you didn't feed illegal Mexican immigrants unless you had to.

Now this act has become another major contradiction on the changing border—catch, incarcerate, and keep "illegals" out of the country. As you do this, though, you should feed them because they are hungry. Let the food money trickle into local outlets, which stay happy and open. It is logical to conclude that restaurants will want those illegal immigrants to keep crossing. Louie Gilot, the reporter, quotes Lucy as claiming that "The agents buy burritos. We have big, jumbo burritos with meat, potatoes, and chile. Sometimes, they get hamburgers and chips and salsa. They really love our salsa. The immigrants must like it because the agents keep coming back."

In George W. Bush's America, more people have been violent against illegal immigrants, and a harsher reality has made it harder to cross, though thousands keep coming. As for Lucy's Mexican Restaurant, the salsa will keep pouring because on the different border of the new century we want to feed everybody, no matter where they come from. Tortillas, beans, salsa, and government dollars are being spent on futilely keeping people out while they pour hot, delicious salsa on burritos from thriving border restaurants.

Everything grows through the corn. It applies to the wound and the crop of injunctions, forested backdrops against the tired praise that will teach me the melody of going up, past the different border of my old and new worlds. Everything grows through the corn. This means that what is not human defies the power of the sun, until the closest, hungriest humans can't destroy themselves without picking the strongest tortured woman out of the field. Everything is harvested like corn. This means the hard, dry husks are nestled in the hair of the woman who smells like grasshoppers, the last aunt who guarded the soil after the crop was destroyed by too much hunger.

The big blue tortilla rolls out of the blue corn to form a flat disc the hands leave alone. The blue tortilla is warm and smells like the hair of the baker and her brown, sweating back, the way she commands the stove. The tortillas stack themselves, the tower growing like in a dream where the cook climbed, then fell into a basket of blue before being buried years later with a full stomach. The big tortilla floats around a bowl of beans before dissolving in a juice that drips off the fingers to streak the table and bless a place for the waiting mouth. The blue tortilla is eaten without asking for a second, its few pieces filling the body with hunger, the last mouthing of something never served.

I found a flower after those last pieces and gave it a kiss, saw alligator cakes with candy teeth waiting in the bakery. Walking through the small village north of Mesilla, New Mexico, I found a locomotive made of sand and stepped on it. A brown recluse spider landed on my big toe, and I let it dance without biting me. The smell of rice filled my stomach with leaves, but I discovered I was not the same hungry man who ate in that bakery, chasing sweet alligators as I tipped my hat to the sun. I drank hot chocolate and fell down a deep well, where I fed myself like a child and told myself I could have whatever I wanted before someone would come along and rescue me.

The abandoned spider web of the brown recluse hangs somewhere in the house, and it might get me when I lie down. Red-breasted birds hover above my hanging plants on the porch, peck at the vines, and take something away. I don't think it is a secret, but can't make myself repeat the old story of wings. Coffee, eggs, waffles, and Thai peppers swallow me—I can't eat them this morning because they fill me with days of masking hunger with my favorite food, until I mold a bread to demolish everything I need.

A friend once told me he entered a small village in southern Mexico where people raised tiny, bald dogs as food. They kept them in pens, slaughtered them, then cooked them into one of the finest delicacies he has ever had. He said he wakes at night sometimes and hears a whimpering, a growl—a barking that says every gnawed bone will be missing when they exhume his grave.

The power of skeletons came to me when I ate a bowl of menudo, the steam vanishing into a mist that let me devour the posole and *chile piquin,* until my stomach burst with the river of menudo. It had to do with falling into a cistern of tripe and the angry red soup of deep change. No one found me when I drowned inside the bowl of menudo. I stopped eating it for years when I saw how the red nipple of the menudo god was the stolen kiss of the man who destroys intestines to gain more than one life.

Not long after that, I dreamed I saw the outstretched hand come out of the bowl of beans and touch my frozen, parted lips, my awe and disbelief the smell of fresh beans and hunger that invented my fear. The hand and arm were brown, and I thought of my mother, but she was buried in sorrow, her years of sweating over stoves and feeding her children where we were poor and alone. The hand that rose out of the beans pushed my chin, then vanished quickly into the hot mound. It was a man's hand, its labor broken at the knuckles, embedded in hard fingers that came out to fill me with the need to be touched, even on the chin, reminding me that men who can afford to feed beans to their children are fathers who lie hidden within the meal, suffocating on the other side of labor, buried in every plate of food eaten by their children over the years.

After a plate of beans, loneliness and ice cream are perfect. They drip down my hands, and I want to tell the one I love that we are still awake—the bed is not completely filled with leaves. This is the way we separate salt from the skin, how we teach each other the arrogance of silence. Tonight I can follow my feet and recall it was a child, years ago, who told me I had four legs. I once saw my grandmother twist a chicken's head right off its flapping body. She sliced the cactus afterwards, cooked the greens to prove there is always healing. I want to remind the one I love that we listen to voices at night after we eat our quiet meal. I remind her she told me there was that shadow by her bed when she was three years old. We know who it was and how he got there.

Tonight, chocolate on my fingers reminds me of the mud that seeped out of my mother's lap. As I and the one I love fall asleep, I don't recall what year it was or how it happened. As we try to dream, we are already there with full stomachs, one footstep ahead of loss, one heel print in front of reason.

Armed vigilante Minutemen patrol the border to make sure no one crosses into the United States illegally. Then the Department of Homeland Security decides that by 2008 passports will be required by those who wish to cross between the United States, Canada, and Mexico. A few months later, this outrage is shot down in Congress, although in the current anti-immigrant atmosphere I believe such a law will be enacted. It would be further proof that the monumental changes this country has experienced since September 11, 2001, are still having an impact on people's lives. For residents along international borders, the possible future requirement of having to get a passport means they would be taxed for living in a region with economic and cultural dynamics created by a vibrant union between countries. Despite the negative aspects of a changing border I have described here, these perpetual political conflicts can't remove the fact that the El Paso border region is a unique part of the country because it is here that two worlds have come together.

The bilingual character of the border with Mexico would be further separated because people would have to wait months to have their passports approved. The ninety-seven-dollar fee to get a passport processed would be a new border tax that would bring millions of dollars to a government who would collect it in the name of tighter security. It would force people to get their pictures taken because the immigration policies of this administration have failed. It is easier to demand personal identification of its citizens and to mask failed policies with a call for passports than to guard nuclear power plants, vulnerable seaports, and railroad lines. It is easier to get a U.S. Customs officer to stare at you to verify your face is actually on your passport than to increase security funding for cities like New York. What about the millions of people who will not be able to afford to get a passport? Where should they line up? Like many things in the Bush era, even the crossing of international boundary lines is a case of have and have not. It hasn't happened because the threatened requirement was cancelled, but in light of the fresh plans to build the border wall it will happen, and so the different border is dark.

This growing void between classes of Americans is not a price that has to be paid for September 11. It is an excuse to impose tighter control over a region that quite often is not in line with the Bush conservative curtain, even if the region can be found on an election night map as lying in several "red states." The dangerous Minutemen are a visually dramatic example of citizens who claim they are doing their part to safeguard the country against terrorists, as they play out their dreams of taking the law into their own hands when it comes to illegal immigration. Armed vigilantes fit into the game plan for the border. If you want to cross illegally, guns will be waiting. If you want to cross the right way, make sure your passport is stamped and your check for ninety-seven dollars is good at the bank.

These barriers do not take into account daily jobs, cross-border commerce, or economic interaction between two countries. How many lawmakers in Washington know how family and business relationships between El Pasoans and people in Juárez work? Who is going to identify how many terrorists were kept out of the United States because they didn't have a passport? When will the U.S. Border Patrol admit that testosterone-healthy men with rifles in Arizona are making government agents' job more difficult as the risk of a major border incident grows? By claiming tighter security as a reason for its actions, the current administration is accelerating the failure of more businesses, restaurants, and retailers. It is turning its back on the fact that cities on both sides of the border depend on each other.

On a recent visit to El Paso, I see that news stories continue to appear about the growing tensions on the border. The Minutemen and their opponents have rallied their forces across the border region several times in 2005, squaring off on the immigration issue and refocusing attention on border policy questions and decisions that need to be made on a national level. I drive around El Paso as these forces gather for conflict and quietly watch my hometown; it looks exactly like that—my quiet hometown. The mobilizations of the Minutemen have come on the heels of figures that reported an all-time high of more than 400 deaths of migrants attempting to cross the U.S. border from Mexico during the U.S. government's fiscal year, which ended on September 30. Border tension also intensified after the U.S. Congress's approval of the Homeland Security bill to increase U.S. Border Patrol personnel by 1,500 agents. Chief among the hotspots for border mobilizations is the El Paso–Juárez–southern New Mexico border corridor, a big region where the number of individuals detained by the U.S. Border Patrol has increased from 104,399 people in fiscal year 2004 to more than 120,000 in fiscal year 2005.

Texas Minutemen, tracked by observers from the American Civil Liberties Union, deployed in early October 2005 on public and privately owned land southeast of El Paso–Juárez and in the Fabens–Fort Hancock region, a popular Texas border-crossing zone for undocumented workers. I drive to Mesilla, New Mexico, one of my favorite getaways in the southern part of the state, only to hear a radio report that a Minutemen group, New Mexico Border Watch, was reported patrolling the southern New Mexico border. As I turn into the ancient town square of Mesilla, I gaze out my car window, expecting to spot one of them on horseback at any second. Of course, questions come up about how closely the Minutemen work with the U.S. Border Patrol.

In 2005, UTEP, my alma mater, debated free speech by forming a faculty committee to study it. At the same time that it was dealing with internal problems with student organizations on campus, a Chicano activist and legendary figure passed away in Denver, Colorado, on April 12. Rodolfo "Corky" Gonzalez died at the age of seventy-six and left behind a legacy of activism from which UTEP students and administrators could learn. Corky was the author of "Yo Soy Joaquin," an epic poem that ranks as one of the two most important and influential works on social justice, along with the late El Paso native Abelardo Delgado's poem "Stupid America." These poems should be required reading by UTEP students and faculty who are waking up to the fact that in George Bush's America free speech and academic freedom are under constant attack. Corky's struggle to preserve dignity among Colorado's Chicano community went on for decades in a state that made news throughout 2005 with attempts to fire Native American activist writer and professor Ward Churchill from the faculty at the University of Colorado. His crime? He exercised free speech by writing about September 11 and questioning who the bad guys were. In these times, when individual liberties are being threatened by forces outside and within our country, universities and higher education are often the first to be targeted.

I wonder how many UTEP students of the campus organizations that were being pressured not to conduct political activities on campus know about Corky's life in Denver. In the 1960s, he formed the Crusade for Justice, an organization that united Chicanos against Denver's notorious police brutality and discrimination. In 1970, he established Escuela Tlatelolco, an alternative school for Chicano students that operates to this day. Like farmworker advocate Cesar Chavez, Corky fought in the trenches, marched, and was arrested more than once. In Denver, after a series of local bombings of Escuela Tlatelolco and numerous internal struggles with other activists, the Crusade for Justice declined. The peak of Corky's political career and of the Chicano movement came when delegates from seventeen states met in El Paso for La Raza Unida's party convention of 1972. Leadership battles went on to destroy La Raza, but Corky continued his work in Denver for several more years. By studying what Corky accomplished in a difficult era, UTEP students would be able to negotiate with the university administration from a stronger position, and current issues over free speech might get a fair review. They would learn that you must remain united and use your academic liberty to fight repressive institutional policies that deny students their basic rights as Americans.

Many El Pasoans have forgotten the infamous, though brief, takeover of the UTEP administration building by Movimiento Estudiantil Chicano de Aztlán (MEChA) students in the early 1970s. Back then, I was an undergraduate at UTEP and have never forgotten the image of El Paso police officers handcuffing Chicano students and throwing them into their patrol cars. Those were different times, but to many of us these days are similar. Recent disciplinary action taken by UTEP against several student organizations that were exercising free speech brings back memories of the 1960s and 1970s, when many people didn't know who their friends or enemies were. Questionable decisions by UTEP took place in a region already under pressure from external forces trying to change the quality of life along the border. That my alma mater has joined in the current atmosphere of repression is pathetic and sad. Corky's death is a timely reminder that the concept of Chicanismo, whether it is spiritual, political, or, to some people, dated, is also a life-long commitment to living your life as a free American. In my public role as a university professor, I know that the best example of this freedom begins academically.

El Paso Times, April 8, 2004
PAINTBALLS FIRED INTO JUÁREZ COMMUNITY FROM UNITED STATES

In Anapra, one of the poorest neighborhoods in Juárez, Mexico, across the border from El Paso, residents claim that they are being shot at with paintballs from the United States. On the night of Monday, April 5, the attackers hit two children and three pregnant women. One child was hit in the face, near his eye. The shootings take place at night and Anapra residents say their attackers use laser scopes and night vision gear. They dress in black so as not be easily spotted. *El Diario* reports that they use a tan-colored truck to get into position on a nearby hill. Anapra residents say that the Border Patrol has seen the paintball shooters and has done nothing to stop them. One Anapra resident told *El Diario* that neighbors "will respond" if the harassment does not stop soon.

The paintball explodes on the stray dog in yellow blood, its howls mistaken for the observant coyote in the hills. The paintball flattens against the pregnant woman in blue streaks, the shade of blue impacting on how her baby will be born, live, and die. The paintball kisses the adobe walls and spills letters in an alphabet more villagers understand than the black-and-white graffiti of their long-lost gang. The paintball flies in the heat before opening in a geometric shape that changes the face of the child into an image any border justice organization would fight to place on their Web site. The paintball stings the brown back of the shirtless boy with a green star that will form a scar he can never wash off.

The paintball buzzes through the swarm of flies circling the outdoor latrines, its impact against the stall sending the insects into an orange frenzy. The paintball electrifies the Mexican flag in the plaza with a purple haze that gathers a crowd around the flagpole in the morning.

The paintball miraculously bounces off the baby in the arms of the woman before disintegrating in a pink cloud that gives the clay jars on the well a Wal-Mart competitive design. The paintball zooms into the eye of the innocent old man, the last thing he sees turning red as if red is the only color he remembers from those days in San Luis Potosí when his mother took him to the wall of roses and showed him where his father died. The paintball blends with the olive green Border Patrol van, whose driver mistakes the impact for a bullet and is shocked that the illegals crossing the river are finally armed. The paintball destroys the statue of la Virgen de Guadalupe, its power cracking the figure's right arm as the film of unknown color wraps the statue in a light many worshippers have been praying for. The paintball decorates the door of la Bruja, the town witch emerging into the night with a crooked stick tied in multicolored ribbons that send the shooters scrambling into their van.

The paintball illuminates the border in a storm of bees, the shooters running out of balls as dawn arrives to give birth to the sparkling, broken windshield on their van, the last two boys they targeted holding the warm pistol between them, their three bullets escaping into the air without giving a clue as to what color could describe them best. The empty paintball cases add color to the desert, the rainbow dirt washed by the next sandstorm into the Rio Grande, whose radioactive waters offer more colors than the latest version of the game.

How to Treat People Who Have Harmed You

I encountered the poor Indian woman sitting on the sidewalk outside the Mexican restaurant and gave her five bucks out of surprise and the guilt I swallow each time I visit my hometown, the bright stripes on her dirty skirt spread over her as if her legs were cut off, her dark brown face and long braids the beauty of the beggar woman with no legs I did see in Juárez many years ago, the old one crossing the busy street in a wooden platform with wheels, this younger woman reminding me that the hunger of time is what we consume and ignore as customers in the restaurant toss half-eaten tacos into the garbage, my charity hidden from customers on their lunch hour, my meat from this place not that good, my five bucks clutched in the woman's hands as she rises and says, "Gracias." She limps away to meet a small boy who was hiding between parked cars. He turns to me briefly and stares as she takes him by the hand. It is the same look I got from the waiter when I ordered the spiciest chili, and my mouth burns from that taste as I follow the woman and boy until I find my car in the packed rows. I sit inside my vehicle for several minutes in the heat, as if sweating the chili inside the car will cleanse my guilt. The sweat runs down my forehead.

Answer the question and you will be fine. How did you tell the difference between water and fire? What did you eat at the table, and how did it taste? Was your father there, and what did he say to your mother? On the day you were born, the leaves were full of rain. In the hour you opened your eyes, the trees were cleared. Place your hands on your lap and love the breeze. The sin of biting and tasting is memory. Rise from the table and go away. There are others here, and their anger splits the stem down to the black seeds, the smelly peels—fruit that is no longer fruit as you return to the room. Answer the question and give them riddles. Ask them what happened to the pet pigeon that limped into their arms when you were five. How did it die? What did you name it? Why did you keep it in a box, hoping it would heal before you changed your mind? It is invisible now with your fear of wings, the snapping bite of the apple set back on the table, a smell of bananas from the highest ferns that hid your father when he had to flee.

Mother, let me remind you how often you told me to turn the other cheek and let the world slap me, as if allowing it was a thing of beauty. Who taught you the scars on your body are the trails left by the blind fingers of those whose duty was to punish you? Let me show you the mimosa tree in your yard that has no marks, only the blossoms from the days of a pure alphabet taught by a mother to her only son. When your father died, you were eleven and you lay in his deathbed and watched his mouth bleed. When did you describe this to me? How long ago did I realize that final embrace between father and daughter would lead to this? Let me tell you how long it has been since the desert wept its punishing rains. Let me give you back the gift of seeing behind the sun, knowing what lies inside the heart, which river leads to the owl waiting in the cottonwood tree. Never cook again for me. The meals a son wants are never served on the dishes set out for him.

The used Chevy I first learned to drive in sits in the ghost lot where my father worked for twelve years as a used-car salesman. On the first day of my new job as the lot boy, I had no choice but to jump in and start the engine because warming up the cars every morning was a crucial part of my duties. I forced myself to drive stick shift this way. One morning, trying to start a standard-gear car, I jerked the clutch, and it jumped into reverse and hit the back of a customer's parked vehicle. No one noticed because the salesman in the lot, not my father, was showing the driver a fancy Oldsmobile on the other side of the huge place. I quickly parked my car, got out, and hurried to a different row of unstarted engines. I was at least twenty cars away, busy wiping the interior of a car, when the customer threw a fit at the dents in his bumper. They never found out who did it.

My job of washing, cleaning, and vacuuming about fifty cars a day kept me inside each one during the intense heat of summer. I would start them, drive between packed rows of cars no one wanted, then pull into the garage to hose, soap, rinse, and dry them by hand with a chamois. I would return them to their slots in the lines, then proceed to the next one. I climbed into each car that sat all day in the 100-degree heat of June with all the windows raised against rain that never came. The interior was a steaming oven, waves of suffocating heat making me work fast as I wiped the dashboards clean, the sweat pouring down my face and soaking my T-shirt. I washed and washed, even on those rare days when sudden rainstorms wiped out a whole day's work. I had to start over with the first car on the front row at the first corner of the lot where potential customers might notice their next shiny purchase.

Thirty-seven years after my job as lot boy, I drive into El Paso and pass the empty block where the used-car place once stood. The weeds and slabs of concrete that survived the decay of El Paso brings back the image of the last car I ever washed there, a red Mustang my father let me drive home because the boss wanted me to practice being a better driver and a good worker—top expert at scraping mud off wheels so the mean salesmen could see their red, hung-over faces in the rims as they laughed at me and wiped their dirty fingers on the clean windshield, ordering me to start over again.

Once a month he took us to La Riviera, the old Mexican restaurant at the crossroads between Las Cruces and El Paso. My sisters and I could always look forward to a meal there, and it was my chance to eat rainbow trout, a delicacy he introduced me to, my taste for fish an imitation of what he ate at the table. There, I found my liking for fish, ordering what he always ate while my sisters and mother stuck to the Mexican food. I watched him when they brought the two steaming plates of trout, the black heads and fins still on them, his skill at pulling the spine and tiny bones out of the delicious meat a careful method I quickly learned. I did what he did—peeled the skin back, cut the head with a fork, and set it aside, delighted at the miracle of being able to lift out the bony spine in one motion. Once a month I shared fish with my father, watched the waiter take away the empty dishes with the white skeleton remains of our sharing piled on top. No one in the family said anything when we were done, my sisters and mother as content with their enchiladas as the men were with the seafood. We all were full and happy, the smell of our meal hanging in the air when, one time, I asked my father, "Where is the rainbow on the fish?"

For my fifth-grade talent show, I learned to play a plastic kazoo as part of a trio with Byron Alexander and Kenneth Korn. We had two weeks to learn three songs whose notes came in the cardboard boxes containing the cheap instruments, kazoos we bought for four dollars at the local Woolworth's. Kenneth was the leader, and we got together at his house several times to practice and go over our routine. I had never played a kazoo before, having rejected my awful experience with trying to learn the trumpet for the fourth-grade school band the year before.

Of course, I was the slowest member of the trio and kept covering the wrong holes on the tiny instrument as we practiced "Long, Long Ago" and "Mary Had a Little Lamb." We had to do the songs over and over until I got it right. We practiced three songs, though I can't recall the name of the third one. Our act of blowing into these odd-looking whistles would be given time to do only three numbers.

Two days before the talent show, Kenneth decided we had to dress up for our performance. He and Byron had sports coats they must have worn to church on Sunday. I did not own such clothes and would be lucky to find a nice pair of dress jeans. We decided on white shirts, black pants, ties, and sports coats. We wanted to look like a professional trio of musicians. When I told my mother that evening about the clothes, we panicked over my wardrobe. She dug through my closet and found a white shirt I had not worn since my first communion. The dark jeans we rooted out were tight and barely covered my ankles. The big problem was that I did not have any dress shoes, a tie, or a sports coat, having rejected the notion of owning any since I was so attached to my dirty white sneakers and faded Levis.

My mother went out and bought me a new pair of shiny black shoes the night before the talent show. Kenneth, Byron, and I managed to practice one more time in the midst of getting our stuff together. Of the three of us, I was the worst musician and kept forgetting the notes and had trouble memorizing which holes to plug with my fingertips as I blew into the red plastic. I did the best I could, but was worried more about my outfit than about playing the right notes. After two weeks of sloppy practices, I knew that Byron and Kenneth were better players and that their loud notes would easily cover up my mistakes. Several times I practiced covering the holes with my fingers and faking the actual blowing of air into the whistle. This way, if I messed up, I was basically miming the playing of the instrument. Brilliant musical style.

The night of the talent show arrived, and the trio was ready. I was nervous that school day, but it went by quickly as different students bragged about what they were going to do that night. I ate dinner quickly as my mother told me for the tenth time to make sure my clothes were ready. I found the neatly pressed slacks and shirt in the closet and got dressed. I grabbed the new pair of shoes in my hands and ran to the waiting car in my sneakers. She drove me to the school. As we approached the parking lot, I was surprised to see many cars and dozens of parents streaming into the school. It made me more nervous, and I told my mother to stop the car. I didn't want my classmates to see my mother driving me to the talent show. She rarely attended school events and had decided not to come to this one. She stopped the car in the middle of the lot. I grabbed my whistle from the seat and hustled out.

My class put on a great show. Two students played the piano, one did magic tricks, and a girl I had a crush on danced to mariachi music. The act right before our trio consisted of four guys—John, Randy, Gary, and Tom—imitating the Beach Boys. They came out in their white- and gray-striped, short-sleeve shirts and mimed a couple of hits while somebody played the records through a loudspeaker. As Byron and Kenneth peeked at the quartet through the backstage curtains, I stood behind them waiting. Kenneth gave us the signal to get ready because the last Beach Boys song was coming to an end. The two of them looked sharp in their coats and ties, with me the odd man out in my white shirt, black slacks, and—my sneakers! I looked down at my feet and it hit me. I had left my new shoes in my mother's car! Even though I had defied Byron and Kenneth by not wearing a coat and tie, there was no way I was going to appear on the auditorium stage in my dirty sneakers. The place was packed with parents, teachers, and students. Without telling my band mates, I yanked my sneakers off my feet, hid them behind a back stage chair, and waited in my black socks. They blended with my pants and would not stand apart from the black shoes Byron and Kenneth wore.

We got our signal from Mrs. Bridler, our teacher, and we bounded onto the stage. A spotlight blinded me as the three of us came forward and stood together in the middle of the platform, Bryon and Kenneth on either side of me. It was a perfect arrangement I created simply by squeezing in between them. It worked because as we started our first song, I forgot the notes. The audience quieted, not knowing what to expect as the guys in coats and the white-shirted one in the middle raised their bright red whistles to their lips and started blowing. My partners covered for me as they played loud and hard, while I pretended I was blowing into the thing. I fingered the air holes at will and tried to match their finger movements, my whistle totally silent. They never turned to look. I thought I heard a couple of giggles, maybe even spotted someone in the darkened crowd pointing at me. Did they notice that the kid without the coat and tie wasn't wearing any shoes? The spotlight glared on the three of us, so there was no way my socks could not be seen. I made it through our ten-minute act, and the three of us bowed and grinned at the thunderous applause. As it died down and we hurried off stage, there was laughter.

Backstage was a different story. Kenneth and Bryon were beaming at each other, but hardly acknowledged me. We had been friends up to then, but they whispered something to themselves as the two of them hurried to find seats out front. They rarely spoke to me after that day. I sat in the folding chair backstage and laced up my sneakers as I caught Mrs. Bridler staring at me from her post near the curtain. In the middle of getting the next batch of kids ready to show their talents, she glared at me.

I didn't stay for the rest of the show. I was suppose to have called my mother to pick me up when it was over, but we lived only three blocks from the school. On this cold November night, I walked home, my white shirt and sneakers shining in the dark, my red whistle stuffed in my pants pocket. When I reached home, I went to the unlocked car before going inside the house and retrieved what I had forgotten on the back seat. I never wore those shiny black shoes.

Putnam Elementary, the school I started attending in 1959 when we moved from central El Paso to the west side, has an infestation of black mold in the spring of 1999. Newspapers report that the school will be shut for weeks as the city tries to get rid of the hazardous bacteria inspectors found on the walls, in closets, in the teacher's lounge, and in the cafeteria. It is everywhere, and hundreds of grade school kids are endangered, which throws parents in neighborhoods around the school into an uproar. I am visiting my hometown when angry parents are interviewed on the five o'clock news. Many decide to keep their children home, some wanting to transfer them to other schools, but experts say that most public schools suffer these sanitation problems. How many more schools will have the dark secrets on their walls uncovered during this scare?

I entered the second grade at Putnam on the first day it opened as a new school. I was in the founding class there and at Moorhead, the new middle school six years later, and then would be part of the first freshman class to go through four years at Coronado High School. Forty years after Putnam opened, I slowed my car as I passed the one-story buildings of the school and recalled how I hated the cafeteria food, was exasperated when I tried to play the trumpet in the band, and was constantly pushed off the monkey bars by the class bullies.

The black mold divides the parents, several of them threatening lawsuits when it is obvious their children have been in danger for a long time. They want to know why the school didn't uncover this problem sooner, and many of them are afraid their children will start dying like flies. The logistical details of sending the students to other area schools during the cleanup fill the news for weeks, the crawling mold stripped of its invisibility as reality catches up with the age of the buildings and takes me to those days when it was a shiny new place. On a second drive past it, I pull to the curve. It is a Saturday, and the empty playground of dirt and gravel looks the same as it did four decades earlier, with the football field the only area with grass, though it is a bright yellow.

I stare at the uncut gridiron and see myself hurrying across it to take a shortcut home. It was November 1963, and I was in the sixth grade, my last year at Putnam. I was eating my lunch with hundreds of other kids in the cafeteria—George Moline, the fattest kid in the school, swallowing his fifth Hershey bar whole as he sat across from me, both of us sweaty from our P.E. exercises on the field. I bit into my egg salad sandwich as George's enormous mouth dripped chocolate and he announced, "They shot President Kennedy." I stared at him, used to his odd behavior, and didn't comprehend what I heard. A gurgling sound came from his throat, and he said it again, "They shot President Kennedy." I noticed several teachers herding their students back to their classrooms as an odd tension filled the lunchroom. The shock fogs the details of the return to my home-room. Mrs. Stocking made us lay our heads on our desks and rest as Mrs. Lindsey, the principal, verified the assassination over the loudspeaker and announced that we were to go home right away. Thirty-eight years later I relive walking down the hot sidewalk, my numbness from a frightening event spreading as I approached my house at the bottom of the hill near the school, my flight from Putnam leading to my first awareness of what America was all about.

Today, black mold releases its microscopic armies into the air of education, kids going to school to learn or not to learn—attending as required because the sanctity of the classroom must survive somehow, whether it is in invisible bacteria or in visible tragedies of gangs and high dropout rates in El Paso. There is black mold in my old school, though the buildings also preserve the triumphs and humiliations I experienced there as a kid, including the talent show. I drive by the school as I leave town and admit that some of my memories are affected by a larger family darkness that reaches beyond historic events, personal histories that my classmates at Putnam might have taken a lifetime to detect. I don't know, though, because I stay in touch with only one friend from those elementary days. The choices that hundreds of others made in living their lives are things I can never know.

Over a span of eight years during the mid-1980s, I did not see or talk to my father. He and my mother divorced in 1982 after thirty-two years of marriage. Since then, visits and conversations have been sporadic, each visit not lasting more than fifteen minutes. Years have gone by without contact. No phone calls and no visits. Since 1996, I have seen my father twice during brief trips to El Paso. Two of the earlier visits were in his office in downtown El Paso when I came to see how he was doing. When I walked into the old brick building, a clothing warehouse he managed, I didn't recognize him. It was 1985 and my first visit to see him after the divorce. The man who rose from behind the desk was bone thin. My father had always been husky and overweight. This man also had long black hair, with thick, wavy curls hanging on his forehead—a contrast to the crew cuts I had known as a boy. My sister Pat had told me our father had picked up the habit of dying his gray hair. The most startling detail I noticed about Ramon Gonzalez was the abundant jewelry, both hands covered with expensive-looking gold and silver rings. A shiny gold chain hung on his neck. He wore a long-sleeved silver shirt, the kind you see men wearing on disco dance floors. I was stunned at the transformation of a fifty-seven-year-old man, even though my mother and sisters hinted that he had really changed since the divorce, in search of his "second youth."

The last time I saw my father before an eight-year stretch of no contact was 1988. It was a brief hello. He came by my mother's house during one of my trips to my hometown. We embraced awkwardly, and he asked me if I needed any money. I shook my head. We both said we were doing fine, and he left. In the 1990s, two or three phone calls per year lasted about five minutes each before he hung up. We exchanged awkward hellos and how's-it-goings. Then, his familiar, "Good talking to you. I'll call you." Click, but no call unless I took the initiative. Each time I called him, he asked for my phone number, explaining he lost it and needs it so he can call me. During my last few visits to El Paso, I have made attempts to see my father. A couple of times I couldn't get a hold of him because he and his second wife move quite often from house to house around town. Other attempts to see him have ended in frustration when he has not shown up at the place we have agreed to meet or he has found an excuse of being busy during my brief stays in El Paso. The two encounters since 1996 changed my perception of him because he was no longer that recently divorced man of the 1980s, but a wrinkled old man, a father I barely recognized from rapidly fading memories of childhood.

Since August 1996, I have called him more often and have tried to extend our phone conversations from five or six minutes to at least ten. This is progress because I have more to say to him since that summer visit to my uncle Jose, my father's older brother, in Sacramento, California. I had not seen Jose, his wife, Violeta, or my cousins in thirty years, the last time being in 1964 in El Paso when I was eleven years old. My uncle had been between assignments in the army and had brought his family for a visit to his hometown.

My uncle made the initial contact by calling me in January. I worked at the Guadalupe Cultural Arts Center in San Antonio from 1990 to 1994. One morning I found a phone message in my box that said, "Call Jose Gonzalez, your father's brother," then the number. I was surprised, thinking something bad had happened. I didn't even know where Jose and his family lived. I was nervous, but called him from my office. There was no answer the first time. I tried several times, but didn't reach him until I got home later that day. When he answered, the similarity between his voice and my father's was startling.

"Hey, Ray! This is your uncle Joe. Remember me? I was talking to your father the other day. He sent me a copy of the article. Congratulations!"

I didn't know what he was talking about, but we had a friendly conversation. It was as if we had been talking for years. My father had sent him a clipping from the *El Paso Herald Post*, a review of my book *Memory Fever*, published the previous fall. I was surprised to hear my father had taken the time to contact him about me. As far as I could recall, it was the first time my father had acknowledged my accomplishments as a writer.

My uncle said, "Your father and us are proud of you. When are you coming to Sacramento?"

I was not used to hearing my family talk about me as a writer. My uncle did not know *Memory Fever* contained pieces referring to my parent's divorce and the breakup of our family—portraits less than favorable of my father. As I told my uncle I would send him a copy of the book, I wondered if he would be still be friendly after reading it. The essays that mentioned my parents were clearly slanted in favor of my mother. I painted my father as the bad guy in their troubles, even though my love and longing for him was expressed in compassion for his plight as a very isolated and withdrawn person. In "My Father's Pool Hall," a piece on a failed business my father had in the early 1960s, I wrote:

> By 1966, my father was struggling as a used car salesman, barely bringing home enough money to buy groceries. I didn't know it then, but I believe now that the pool hall was a turning point in my parent's marriage. After the business failed, they worked hard to pay off the debt, the loans, struggling to put food on the table for me and my three sisters. For years after, I watched my father work hard at sleazy used-car lots and waited with my mother, late at night, for him to

come home, exhausted, so she could feed him a late-night dinner. It was the beginning of the end, a crumbling that took almost another twenty years to complete.

Several essays referred to feeling like I lived only half a life in El Paso—one influenced by historical events around my mother's side of the family, but nothing from the Gonzalez side. Her father worked in the Yaqui railroad camps of Arizona before World War I. Her mother, my grandmother Julia, raised me as a baby in El Paso and influenced my religious and spiritual life. The result was a childhood shaped by a dominating mother and a distant, passive father who carried his secrets with him, intimate details of his youth in a small border town in the middle of a vast desert.

One story my father did share when I was a boy was about his having to shine shoes on street corners at the age of five. He told me this several times over the years, emphasizing that he made pennies and nickels from shining the shoes of strangers near the railroad station and outside of dingy bars so he could have money to eat. He claimed his father, Jose Sr., was a miser who threw his kids into the streets to fend for themselves after his wife, Josefina, died. My grandfather Jose also worked for the railroad. My father retold his shoeshine story with pride, reminding me how tough it was for a man to make a good living. I refer to the shoeshine boy in my book. Later, during my visit to Sacramento, my uncle reprimanded me for this, insisting his father had been a generous man who had taken good care of his family. He insisted it was not true that my father had to survive on the dirty streets of El Paso during the 1930s. Jose, the older brother, was responsible for Ramon and said he had taken care of him when their mother died in their youth. This contradiction between the two brothers would not be the first I would find as I learned more about the Gonzalez family.

I promised my uncle that my wife and I would come visit that summer. We ended our conversation with his saying, "It's good talking to you. I've always asked Ray about you. Your cousin Tony said he heard you on the radio a few months ago." It was ironic that he brought up my radio presentation because it was about my father. After *Memory Fever* came out, I was contacted by National Public Radio to do a commentary from my essays. Their editor read my book and asked me to condense "My Father's Pool Hall" to three minutes.

After I hung up, I sat on the living-room sofa and cried. I told my wife, Ida, about my father sending a copy of the review to Jose. I cried because it was a sudden turn in my relationship with my father. I wept because my uncle told me my father was proud of me, something my father could never say to my face. When I had started writing seriously, back in the early 1970s, the only thing I heard from my father was, "When are you getting a real job?" It was a strange sensation to have someone in my father's family talk to me. A certain pressure had been removed. I had not seen my father in years, but there I was talking to his brother, whom I had not seen in thirty. The fact that my uncle took the step of calling created new possibilities. I felt as if my role as my father's son and as a writer trying to deal with the past had widened. It energized and frightened me at the same time. This anxiety had to do with my parents' divorce because I had assumed that my father's adultery was the catalyst for the end to what must have been a miserable marriage. It was a disintegration that for me, as a boy who believed the family circle was utopia, had never been evident. Writing *Memory Fever* helped me understand the mysteries of childhood, but as I got off the phone with my uncle, I knew I had written only half of the story.

The other side was the history of my father's family, about which I knew nothing. It was built around my father's silence and his inability to be close and talk to me. My most vivid memories include his driving us to the movie theater downtown without saying a single word to me. I would sit in the passenger seat and look out the window at the passing cars. We sat in the dark theater without saying a word. I also remember when he tried to make me a baseball player. For several weeks one summer, we played catcher and pitcher. He bought me a glove and ball and made me pitch it to him hard, dozens of times, wanting me to try out for the Little League team as a pitcher. After days of throwing him the ball as he crouched in the catcher's stance, I went out for the team. The coach stuck me in right field, cutting me from the team two days into practice.

One of the most unforgettable memories has to do with the senses, tying into the passage I quoted about my father being a used-car salesman most of his adult life. I can never forget the late nights waiting with my mother for him to come home. He would always show up very tired, eat dinner, and lie down. He would take off his shoes and socks and turn on the late-night television, then I would sit on the edge of the bed and watch TV with him. He would sigh and stare at the black-and-white screen, lying there and not moving as a powerful smell filled the room. To this day, the memory of the tired car salesman brings back the sweaty smell of those shoes and socks. The odor of his feet was overpowering and hangs in my nose as the eternal scent of a man who worked hard, made little money, and grew more distant from his family. I equate the smell with my father's weariness—a lingering cloud I would give anything to experience again because it is both repelling and endearing. I want to sit on the edge of the bed, waiting for him to say something. It is the smell of love, compassion, and distance. It is the odor of men.

My father is guilty of adultery and abandoning his family. He didn't want anything to do with his grown children after the divorce. This has continued for almost twenty-five years after my parents went their own ways. My attempts to start a dialogue and to see him were frustrated by his unwillingness to have a good, postdivorce relationship with his son and daughters. At the time I first talked to Jose, I had no idea the visit to Sacramento would help in trying to break the pattern of being caught between my mother's guilt trips and my father's ignoring me. My uncle's call filled me with anticipation, but also with the fear of being let down again. Even though I looked forward to the trip to Sacramento, I was afraid my uncle would disappoint me, just like my father did. Things had started on a positive note because this contact, after thirty years, had come about from my writing. The day after the phone call I sent several copies of *Memory Fever* to my uncle because my cousins wanted to read it.

I called my father a few days after talking to Jose. The first time, I got the usual answering machine with his wife's voice on it. I had left unreturned messages before, so I hung up on the machine. I got a hold of him the next day, and we had a short talk that I extended by a few minutes when I mentioned my uncle.

"Yeah, I sent him the newspaper," my father told me. "He's always asking me about you. He said Tony heard you on the radio. Send me a copy of your book."

I have dozens of books of poetry by male writers who write about their fathers. Robert Bly is one of the best writers on the topic, and, to some critics, the "father poem" has become a cliché in itself. There are a handful of anthologies of father-and-son poems, one of them publishing a poem of mine a few years ago. It wasn't hard finding something to send the volume's editors because I have written at least one hundred poems about my father. Several appeared in my first two published books of poetry. My third book, *The Heat of Arrivals*, contains a crucial section of nothing but father poems. The central poem in the section "The Energy of Clay" ends with this stanza:

> Of my father, he lives in two worlds—
> land of the digger and the cave of clay,
> territory he never inhabits because
> his houses were built from harder ground,
> mixture of the bitter cottonwood and the thorn,
> formed with the isolation of walls where all fathers,
> in their son's clay, lie down to forget.

My fourth book, *Cabato Sentora*, is centered on themes of building and destroying family myths and how they delay the writer's journey toward understanding where he came from and why he writes. Despite the publication of these books, I am tired of writing father poems. They are a small fraction of the poetry I have written, but are the most disturbing pieces, and the subject keeps emerging when I am in the middle of creating new poems. I can't get away from writing about my father and my family, a dilemma many writers welcome and build careers on, while others struggle to escape it and write about other things. My creative process is ingrained with my past, the continuing family poems perhaps being the lost conversations I never had with my father when he drove us to the movies. They are the shameful words of defense I used to explain why I got cut from the baseball team, the lingering images of an exhausted man whose smelly feet melt into the heat of the desert, until they are molded out of clay by the trembling hands and sharp language of his son.

My wife and I flew to San Francisco and rented a car for the drive to Sacramento. I had been to the Bay Area many times, but never felt as apprehensive as I did that summer. My visit with Jose and his family was a combination of wonderful leisure time playing tourists and intense conversations about my father. Jose is five years older than my father. He is retired from the military after forty years of service and five bullet wounds in his head that he received in three major wars. During one of our talks on his patio, he told me he had killed 82 Japanese soldiers during World War II and 42 North Koreans and Chinese in the Korean War. The figure that made me stare at him for a long time was the 140 Vietnamese men and women he had killed in North and South Vietnam.

Jose showed me dozens of medals he got as a hero. He revealed that he had served in the U.S. Army Special Forces. It is how he tallied 9 Purple Hearts, 5 head wounds, and 264 kills. He told me there are many things he did as a soldier that he can't talk about, but admitted he was a secret U.S. advisor at Dien Ben Phu, the 1954 battle where the Vietnamese defeated the French forces. There weren't suppose to be any Americans in Vietnam during that time. He was also part of the Phoenix Program, in which U.S. Special Forces and South Vietnamese agents killed thousands of Viet Cong and North Vietnamese in the late 1960s. My uncle told me he was so good at his job that he and his partner, working in two-man teams behind enemy lines, had had a high monetary price placed on their heads by the North Vietnamese.

In 1987, after he had already retired, his wounds caught up with him. He was hospitalized with a large brain tumor. He almost died and spent months in the Veterans Hospital in Sacramento. The doctors told him the tumor was caused by the shape his brain was in after five head wounds. My uncle is an intelligent and articulate man. He speaks in a normal voice. He is doing fine now and enjoys his retirement. He does volunteer work at a number of charities in Sacramento.

I describe what I know of his military life because what he told me still shocks me and is a factor in how I see him and my father. In their own distinct ways, they are lonely heroes. My uncle did it for his country and survived. My father, who served in the navy between World War II and Korea, has survived in a less dramatic fashion on the home front. Either way, it seems both of them have played out the lives of two loners. I couldn't have reached these conclusions before my visit to Sacramento. My uncle's experiences in Special Forces and his years spent away from his family tie into the code of silence my father follows. The things my uncle told me about himself gave me the ability to see my father and his family in a more realistic light. After all these years, I made a start in moving out from under my mother's official version of what kind of family the Gonzalez clan was suppose to be. I could love them completely, at last.

My uncle's sad and brutal accounts of his military actions and of how his wife and children went months without knowing what part of the world he was in fit the characteristics of Gonzalez men that are never going to change. While my uncle's January phone call came with great potential, his revelations about his secret life told me to bring him down off the pedestal on which I had placed him after he called me. His forty years of being gone from his family and a certain disturbing pride he expressed in remembering his war tales told me he was not that different from my father. Both of them had lived a major portion of their lives without the immediate love and attention of family. My uncle even told me that during the infamous Cuban Missile Crisis of 1962, he had disappeared for six months without contacting Violeta and his children. Military intelligence didn't allow for such contact. Despite these sobering facts, I knew I had done the right thing in coming to Sacramento. Perhaps there was a growing crack in the code of silence that kept my uncle in military service for so long. If I could have longer phone conversations with my father after Sacramento, it might mean we were weakening the code.

While Ida and I visited, my uncle was very generous. He told me he liked my book, but added that it was very one-sided. I felt self-conscious talking about it. I got excited when he promised me to send me the Gonzalez family tree and other information about how my father's ancestors had settled in New Mexico in the mid–nineteenth century. One evening I asked him about the great-great-grandparents and other family members

I never knew. I took pages of notes. Our talks about the family tree led to conversations about my father.

The day after my uncle told me about his military career, he shared several things about his brother. He said my father had always been very quiet, and it was hard for him to tell me he was proud.

"Did you know Ray had a heart attack in 1988?"

"What?" I shook my head.

"He didn't tell you about it?" My uncle frowned and looked down at his coffee cup. "He was in the hospital for several days."

"No," I swallowed. "I didn't know."

It was shocking and disturbing news because I never knew about it, and neither did my mother and sisters. I could see how such things could happen without anyone from his first family finding out. After the divorce, my father became very good at going for long periods of time without our knowing where he lived or what he was doing.

One of the most memorable conversations Jose and I had was about the two brothers' childhood in El Paso. Jose laughed about how he had always led the way for my father. He had protected him from neighborhood bullies on the streets of El Paso during the Great Depression. Their mother, Josefina, died when my father and Jose were small boys. Jose told me that the day after her funeral, he and my father were walking down a street in south El Paso. They came to a very busy intersection. My uncle took his brother's hand so they could get across the street. As they waited for a chance to cross, Jose looked toward the opposite corner and saw his mother standing there, pointing at her sons. He motioned to his brother. My uncle claims they both saw their mother standing in the middle of a crowd, trying to cross toward them. By the time they stepped onto the busy street and dodged several cars to get across, she was gone.

My uncle swore this incident was true. He told me to ask my father about it sometime. I haven't asked him. I know the ghost of my father's mother has come back because she has appeared in several of my poems. I have written about her because I have dreamed of her. I always know who she is, even though I never knew her. These dreams occur every now and then. So far, they all have taken place before my trip to Sacramento and my uncle's story. The grandmother I never knew has appeared in my dreams, just like she appeared to her sons after her death. Perhaps now I know why.

Dreams have dominated my poems for many years. Some of them contain strangers I know are family members from the past. Talking to my uncle gave my family poems a different edge that does not disturb me. A few of the dreams have ended with feelings of suffocation—the distress of a nightmare. I don't know why some of them have concluded in that manner. In some of those dreams, these people are trying to harm me.

My uncle's tale about his mother was one of the last ones he shared before my wife and I returned to Texas. The four days we spent with him went by quickly. There were times during our talks, as we sat at his kitchen table, that I swore I was talking to my father. They look very much alike, even though I can't really say what a man I hadn't seen in eight years looked like at the time. They both have broad foreheads and dark, wavy hair. My father once told me his brother's hair turned completely white after his brain operation. Jose showed us a photo from World War II, when he was twenty years old. He is very thin and looks like Elvis Presley. My wife claims the Gonzalez men have very feminine facial features. The round cheeks and dark eyes run in the family.

We said our good-byes. My uncle invited me and Ida to come back again. I asked her to drive most of the way back to San Francisco because I was weeping. I had not cried that hard over anything in years. The rush of sobs came from the rich information I had gathered about my father and the grief I encountered over his family's past, which had been kept from me. The crying also came from knowing I was ending a part of my isolation. I grieved because I was going to have a different relationship with my mother. She was no longer in control of the official family record. I had to accept that the new relationships I formed with my relatives were not going to bring my father back to me the way I wanted him. It was up to me and my father to do that.

I called him a few days after we returned home. I said how much I enjoyed seeing my uncle. I repeated some of the names he had given me from the Gonzalez family tree. My father remembered some of his ancestors and was curious about others. I told him I found out about his heart attack of a few years ago.

My father paused over the line. "That's not true. I never had a heart attack," he said quickly, then laughed. "Your uncle doesn't know what he's talking about."

He changed the subject to the usual, "I'm glad you're doing OK. Why don't you give me your number so I can call you?" I gave it to him as I had done many times and we said good-bye. Between 1996 and 2006, I have seen my father twice.

Far from the grave, your father still loves you. As you open a book of your poems, a photo you took of him drops out. You had forgotten you had placed it there—his wrinkled face blaming you instead of the image on the photo that never moves. What is this? A photo of a father in his son's book of poetry. The old man leans against his new car, trying to smile. He manages a wrinkled smirk because he is being photographed by a son he has not seen in eight years. There is a brief lunch at a Chinese restaurant, followed by a package in the mail for Christmas—a yellowing hardcover he bought at a Goodwill Store to send to his writer son as a gift. It is a very old copy of a turn-of-the-century anthology called *America's Best-Loved Poems*. This makes you put your book down and close it without reading your own writing, wondering if you have written the accurate thing. Is he staring at you in the photo, trying to tell you that his favorite poem of yours is not included in the ancient book?

The transformation from speaking my native Spanish to the shocking necessity of speaking English happened when I was five years old. Until then I spoke only Spanish at home, even though my parents were bilingual and I heard them speak English. My grandmother Julia, who raised me during those first years, could not speak English, so Spanish was what I heard all day. Going to a Catholic school from kindergarten through first grade changed everything and added additional pressure. My memories of St. Mary's Catholic Church in downtown El Paso are filled with the strange cruelty of the nuns and how I learned my first words of English.

The nuns beat kids on the head with yardsticks, punishing them by placing dunce caps on their heads and sticking them in the corner. If you got caught chewing gum, it would not go on your nose like it did in public schools, but got stuck to your chin. The guilty students had to sit perfectly still as the wad of gum slowly hung down their chins. As time went on in the hot classroom, the gum would hang farther down until the student was told to remove it with a Kleenex and throw it away. The nuns first job was to make sure no one spoke Spanish in the classroom, in the cafeteria, or on the playground. Speaking Spanish was against the rules and punishable by a beating with the paddle, the whacking sound and cries of the kids followed by the screeching of the nuns, "English only! Do you hear me? English only!" Whack! A few hard blows on your rear and off to your desk. I recall kids sitting at their desks, silent tears streaming down their faces, trying not to sob aloud because any sound meant one more swat to whatever part of their body the nun could hit as they sat there. I never got caught because I was too shy to speak to other kids and couldn't communicate with them because I didn't know English. When I ran into my cousin Benny, who also went to school there, we whispered to each other in Spanish.

English came to me on one day I will never forget. My kindergarten teacher was Sister Irene, a tall, thin nun who reminded me of a stork in the picture books we were given to read. She loved to move the kids around the room all the time. We would be assigned a certain seat, memorize the desk we were to occupy in complete obedience, then she would scramble the seating chart the following week. She never stopped shuffling us around throughout the school year.

That day we had been studying the eight basic colors, and their names were my first attempt in recognizing English words and objects. Sister Irene divided the class of thirty-two kids into groups representing each color, with four of us per color. She had eight huge poster cards painted in the various colors, with the name of the color under each square. When she called my name, she held up the red card. I breathed a sigh of relief because I knew Carlos and Anna, two kids in the red group. By mingling with them, I could hide the fact I didn't know the word *red*. I managed to understand what Sister Irene wanted us to do as we sat quietly at our newly assigned seats.

That week I was in the desk closest to the hallway door leading to the playground. The sister instructed us to stand when she held our color card in front of the class. As she held green, the four kids assigned that color had to rise and repeat the name of the color aloud. We started this game at the end of the school day, and everyone was restless to go home. The sister sometimes had trouble keeping kids from running out the door when the bell rang. Some of us had to catch buses to get home, which was often miles away from downtown. In her heavy Spanish accent, Sister Irene told us to sit quietly so we could begin. She spoke good English. Most of the nuns were from Mexico, though they never said one word in Spanish.

Sister Irene held up the orange card. Four kids stood by their desks and repeated the word *orange* together.

"Very good, Samuel. Yes, Leticia." The sister repeated the name of each group member as he or she answered correctly. She held up green, and the group stood and answered, "Green."

Anticipating my group's turn, I gripped the edge of my desk and stretched my neck to look at the color cards. The sister sat on a stool four rows away. This happened weeks before my parents discovered I needed eyeglasses, an oversight corrected by the second grade. My anxiety grew because the red card had not been held up yet. Tony, a kid behind me, whispered in Spanish that the final bell was going to ring in five minutes.

I nodded in silence. There were three colors left, including my red. Sister Irene held up the blue card, and I quickly stood with the four kids in the blue group. Laughter broke out across the room, jeers and calls against me growing louder. I was frozen by my desk and could not sit down. Sister Irene's menacing look was shocking and caused sweat to run down my forehead.

"No, Ramon! You are in the red group! Red!" She yanked the red card from her lap and showed it to me. When the laughter died down, she said, "Ramon, you stay after school until you learn your colors. Sit down."

I became dizzy and almost fell into my seat. I did not know what the phrase "stay after school" meant, though I sensed it was bad by the looks I got from the kids seated around me. I had never stayed after school before and would miss my bus. My older cousin would not wait for me, and I didn't know the bus schedule to catch a later one. There was no such thing as a school bus in a Catholic school in El Paso in 1956.

The sister held up the yellow card after the blue. I watched the four kids get up through the haze of tears in my eyes as Tony behind me explained my punishment in Spanish. I whispered to myself, "Yellow." The final card was mine, and I stood and croaked the word *red* with my group. The sister acknowledged all four of us for standing on red.

Suddenly, the bell rang and startled me. Students grabbed bags and coats as they headed for the door. The sister was surrounded by dozens of excited kids and did not see I was the first to exit. I ran across the schoolyard in terror and did not look back. I found my cousin, and we boarded the bus. It pulled away as I sat in the huge seat and turned around to look toward the school. All I could see were hundreds of kids pouring out of the building.

I don't recall how I slept that night, but it must have been awful. I had to go to school the next day and face the consequences of disobeying Sister Irene. I got on the bus that morning in a frightened daze, wondering how many swats I would get. Nothing happened. The sister forgot she told me to stay after school. None of the kids mentioned it to her. My mistake of standing on the color blue, instead of on red, was forgotten overnight. I spent the day in careful fear, but made it to the final bell. I pulled out my box of eight crayons and repeated the eight colors to myself several times that day. I even did it during lunch where I sat in the stuffy, basement cafeteria eating the egg salad sandwich my mother prepared for me every single day.

I held the eight crayons in one hand, set my egg salad sandwich on the table, and turned to Benny. He stared at me as I switched each crayon from my left hand into my right. I correctly said, "Red, blue, green, purple, brown, black, yellow, and orange." Those were my first words in English.

My father used to take me to Juárez to get a haircut. As an eight-year-old, I dreaded the way the Mexican cutters mishandled me on the barber's chair, jabbing my ears with their scissors or shaving my hair too short with their faulty electric razors. The chair swiveled rapidly as they worked me over, and I would get quick glimpses of the huge barbershop packed with customers and barbers smelling of cheap aftershave and those mysterious smells that packs of men give off when they are trying to look handsome together.

The worst part came when the barber led me to the sinks in the middle of the long room and dunked my head in hot water to wash my hair before cutting it. I was shocked by the plunge into the steaming mixture of shampoo and tap water, then came up gasping as the barber gripped my neck and dug his knuckles into my scalp, making sure the grime of a childhood in the desert came off. Seen without my eyeglasses, the rows of chairs looked like white ghosts, customers draped in white sheets, the barbers outfitted in blue-and-white uniforms—a chatter of Spanish rising in volume as old friends walked in and old friends tipped their cutter generously on the way out, dirty jokes and curse words reverberating through the metallic applause of scissors that kept a clipping rhythm throughout the place.

My father knew several of the barbers well, and Chucho was a favorite of his—the man's huge stomach pressing against the back of the revolving chair as he ran his electric razor over my father's head to shape the perfect crew cut. One time I stumbled blindly from the sinks with soap in my eyes, my barber pausing in the crowd to talk, leaving me to find my way back to my chair. Unable to see without my glasses and suffering watery eyes, I ran into Chucho cutting my father's hair. The fat man, who wore his hair in a greased ducktail, laughed at me and said something to my father above his whirring razor. My blindness must have been obvious because both men pointed me down the foggy aisle of occupied chairs. I don't know how long it took to get back to mine, but the shock of tripping over cowboy boots and freshly shined leather shoes as they stuck out into the aisle on foot rests told me I was in a world of men that had its distinct space and way of doing things.

My barber returned, laughing at something and muttering Spanish words I didn't understand. He wiped my head roughly one more time, then shocked me again by slapping my face with stinging cologne, though I was too young to shave. I don't know what he spread through my clean hair before starting to cut it, but it burned my scalp. When I was a boy, my parents never allowed me to grow my hair long, so I don't know why the Mexican barbers spent so much time on me. I closed my eyes as the long blades of the scissors clipped the top of my head and the barber pushed my neck forward with his icy fingers to get to the area under my collar.

The electric shavers in Mexican barbershops were always dull; they cut me down to size with a scraping that left my vulnerable scalp sore, but clean. Even though I couldn't see well, one of my favorite things to do—the signal the torture was almost over—was to watch the hairs fall off my head onto the blue-striped sheet in which I was draped. I would squint, and the hairs would come into focus as they landed on my covered chest and arms. When I thought the barber wasn't watching, I would shake the sheet and watch the hair fall to the floor. It was one of the last stages before my glasses were handed back and I had my freedom.

One of my last haircuts in Juárez made me stay away from barbershops for the rest of my life. I swear I have not gone into one on either side of the border since then. As I sat covered in the sheet, blurry shapes went through their social rituals across from me. I was starting to get bored when I felt my barber get very close to the back of my head—an unexpected slip of his rhythm. I jumped as his scissors cut the top of my ear. I had been nipped before, but this was the worst; blood started pouring down the left side of my neck onto the white sheet. Even without my eyeglasses, I could see the huge bloodstains. The barber quickly twirled my chair to face him. I don't remember what he looked like because I was stunned by the blood. He grabbed a steaming hot towel from a warming tray and held it against my ear. This caused further pain, and I cried out. My father must have been sitting in the next chair because his large figure quickly appeared. As the barber removed the bloody towel, my father dabbed my ear with a cotton ball, and both men laughed. The barber splashed a green, smelly paste on my ear, and the pain almost threw me out of the chair.

I pulled the blood-stained sheet off me and did the one thing I could never do in front of my father—I ran out of the crowded barbershop, having grabbed my glasses and a couple of cotton balls from the counter. I leaned against our parked car down the street, held the cotton to my bleeding ear, and waited for my father, who took forever to come out. By the time he finished his haircut, a shave, and plenty of socializing, my ear had stopped bleeding.

I shall always associate the smell of cheap cologne with my father's car and the fact that he rarely spoke to me when we went somewhere together. He certainly didn't say a word as we waited in heavy traffic to cross the international bridge back to El Paso. It was hot that day, and I kept rolling the windows down to get the smell of the barbershop out of the vehicle. I don't think it went away because the presence of a silent father and his son returning from being cut in a fine Mexican barbershop hung in our house for a long time.

Turn it down! Turn it down!
—bar crowd on "Voodoo Chile"
from Jimi Hendrix's *Electric Ladyland*

It is 1967, and I am hung up on the Beatles. My cousin Tony lives in England because my uncle Joe, a military lifer, is stationed there. Tony keeps writing me about all these strange British bands I've never heard of—Pink Floyd, John's Children, the Incredible String Band. The first British record he finally sends me, instead of just writing about it, is a sleek 45 rpm single by some band called the Jimi Hendrix Experience. He wants me to listen to the main song, "Hey Joe," which hasn't hit the United States yet. I listen to it and think the band sucks. What is that awful singer saying about a "gun in your hand?" Give me back "A Hard Day's Night." One day, without noticing, I put the flipside on my portable stereo, a song I'd never played called "51st Anniversary."

I start the thing, and the explosion of cosmic guitar and beautiful voice give me my first rock-and-roll anxiety attack! I can't believe it. I'm fourteen years old, and I've gone to music heaven. "I'm gonna change your mind!" the singer screams. Jimi Hendrix? The singer? He must be the guitarist. Is he the leader? I'm used to thinking of rock bands as whole groups like the Beatles, no individuals or solo musicians standing out. I have no idea who Bob Dylan is yet. It is too early for John Lennon's rebellion. I play "51st Anniversary" all day, the short song fading away, only to be revived when my shaking arm places the heavy needle back at the beginning. Within two months, I've scratched the 45 and have been desperately searching the Woolworth's for the Jimi Hendrix Experience's first album. Nothing. No one has ever heard of the band or the record.

My cousin in London is way ahead of me because they get all the new psychedelic music before we do in the States. All I can do is wait. Months later, I walk into Woolworth's, and there it is—three wild-looking guys in a circular frame on the cover. I grab the album and search the playlist on the back. "51st Anniversary" is not listed! The song is not included on the U.S. version of the album, and I want to cry right there in the Woolworth's. I drop the record in the racks and walk out. My record collection begins to grow—Buffalo Springfield, the Who, Fever Tree, the Grateful Dead, and my favorite American band at the time—Jefferson Airplane. One day, in the middle of the Dead's "New, New Minglewood Blues," I search my record shelf for the Hendrix 45 because I haven't played "51st Anniversary" in weeks. I shuffle through the albums and the metal rack where I keep other 45s and can't find the gift from Tony. "51st Anniversary" is gone. Someone has taken my only copy of an obscure song that I can't even have on their first record, but it is weird because I'm the only one in my family who loves rock music. My mother and three sisters would never touch my record collection. I never see the 45 again.

Thirty-five years later I can still see the shiny silver label on the beautiful British vinyl that always sounded better than U.S. copies. I see that precious collector's item every time I play "51st Anniversary" off the latest Jimi Hendrix CD, but where is my lost 45? I share this story with my cousin Tony, now a lawyer in St. Louis, and he tells me that his copy vanished in London as well. I ask him to repeat what he just said. "My copy of '51st Anniversary' disappeared around that time," he says, "but I went out and bought another one. In England, you could get one easily." He adds that a Hendrix fanatic in the United States once showed him a list of rare Hendrix items on the collector's market and pointed to Reprise 0597—the British 45 of "Hey Joe/51st Anniversary" released in 1967 with a picture sleeve. Today's collector's price for that single—$1,000. It is my missing 45, and I had the one with the picture sleeve of the band. I even pinned it above my bed for a few weeks as I kept wearing out "51st Anniversary." I ask Tony what happened to his copy in England. "I don't know," he says on the phone. "I used to play it over and over, and one day it was gone. But I had hundreds of records." So did I, and we both moved on.

From *Goldmine Magazine* no. 525:

When her acting career started to fade, Hollywood sex blonde Jayne Mansfield attempted to sing pop singles. Sometime between October and November of 1965, record producer Ed Chalpin used session player Jimi Hendrix for a session with Mansfield. Hendrix played bass and then added guitar to Mansfield's vocal tracks on two songs—"As The Clouds Drift By" and "Suey." While traveling to fill in for the stage version of *Gentlemen Prefer Blondes*, Mansfield was decapitated in a car accident on June 29, 1967. "As The Clouds Drift By" b/w "Suey" was released on July 7th. These two of the rarest Hendrix pre-Experience tracks were released in 1994 on the CD *Jayne Mansfield Too Hot to Handle*. There was a rush on buying it by thousands of Hendrix collectors. There is no mention of Jimi Hendrix on the credits.

In May 1970, three of my high school friends in El Paso invite me to go to the first Denver Rock Festival with them as a graduation present to us all. Denver is seven hundred miles to the north. I turn down the chance to go because my summer job washing used cars in the 105-degree heat of the asphalt lots has started and I need the one-dollar-per-hour wages. Two weeks later my friends return from Denver with shocked looks on their faces because they were teargassed by Denver police at Mile High Stadium.

The festival erupted into a riot, but they claim they saw Jimi Hendrix right before the chaos. Despite the festival's falling apart, it would have been my one and only chance to see him.

> I am your trash man / I come to keep your houses clean / I am the trash man / take out all your dirty blues and dreams / Well, when I come around to collect for the bill.
> —Jimi Hendrix, unreleased journal
> from *Cherokee Mist: The Lost Writings*

John, one of my high school friends who was gassed in Denver, returns from his first trip to San Francisco with the British import copy of *Electric Ladyland* under his arm. We sit in his room and stare at the cover with its beautiful and naked, though wasted-looking, British babes. We try to guess which ones Jimi fucked before and after the photo session. The song lineup is the same as on my American version, but we can't get over that cover, though the blazing red-and-yellow silhouette of Jimi's head on the U.S. cover of *Electric Ladyland* is becoming one of the most popular images of Jimi that everybody owns.

> "He could have given that guitar to somebody instead of burning it," Donna admonished. Sterling Morrison of the Velvet Underground once told me the exact same thing.
> —rock critic Tony Nordlie in *Goldmine Magazine* no. 525,
> recalling a 1992 conversation with a girl selling cokes and
> popcorn at a movie theater showing *The Monterey Pop Festival*
> (in 1967, Monterey was the first U.S. performance of the
> Jimi Hendrix Experience, a concert made famous when Jimi
> set his guitar on fire at the end of his performance)

My spinning arms evolve from playing air guitar to taping a yardstick onto a rectangular cigar box. I'm fifteen years old, and the Beatles make me clear my parents' old wooden desk of everything. I jump on it, stand on it like it's my stage, and play my guitar while Robin, my next-door neighbor, spins my latest album, *Beatles 65*, on the turntable. I'm good on "She's a Woman," but great on that cool feedback George Harrison opens with on "I Feel Fine." One day Robin shows up with a forty-dollar Woolworth's guitar his father bought him for his birthday. The problem is he couldn't afford to buy his son the tiny amplifier sold separately, the device about the size of a car battery. Robin outdoes me by using a real guitar pick to strum the quiet strings of the beautiful guitar with its black and deep brown body and light yellow, wooden neck. No electricity. He makes me look like a kid every time we play our Beatle albums and mime the songs on top of the desk. One day the "51st Anniversary" gift from Tony shows up in the mail. I put it on, grab my cigar box guitar, and go wild on the desk, almost falling off a couple of times. Robin has never heard the Jimi Hendrix Experience before and stares at my vibrating stereo speakers. The wild noise destroys our Beatle-buddy thing forever. He unties his strap, grabs his Woolworth's guitar by the neck, and leaves my house. I don't see or speak to him for years.

"Machine Gun"—my cousin Pifas lost in Vietnam. Band of Gypsys wailing through the smoke and fire of a divided country, extending beyond the high school years of my listening to my favorite music and trying to figure out why Hendrix disrupted my habits of playing my album collection. "Woke Up This Morning and Found Myself Dead"—my first Hendrix bootleg vinyl. I find it at Lenny's Records, one of the few head shops in El Paso in the late 1960s. I pay ten dollars for it, buying it two months after Pifas is MIA. One of the worst Hendrix recordings ever, with Buddy Miles, Johnny Winter, and a drunk Jim Morrison. The cover still haunts me. It is a Day-Glo blue with a dancing skeleton on the cover, its headband mimicking Jimi—these wasted rock stars making underground history, the awful sound on the bootleg dark and gloomy as it marks time on my music calendar.

Thirty years later it is the age of the DVD, and rock music has turned to a visual dance, a fire that burns beyond pure sound. We no longer listen to music. We watch it instead. What counts these days is image, the seeing document of sound—the way it was and the way it is now—things that can be seen, not just felt. This means there are at least one-dozen Hendrix videos and remasters on DVD. Jimi and his guitar are everywhere in DVD land, though I wonder how his visuals sell these days. When we can see him on our computers and television screens, it means he has returned in unexpected ways, those colorful outfits and scarves so brilliant, massive, and blinding on our home-theater, surround-sound systems. His career is now highly documented as a visual display of sheer electric guitar dynamics. The Hendrix family took over a few years ago and recharged his legacy, bringing it into the modern musical technology that feeds fanatical music historians like myself, but how many young music lovers, raised on MTV and now on DVD, are going to allow Jimi's image to overcome their passion as fans?

I begin the semester by playing Jimi at Woodstock for my "Literature of Rock and Roll" class, perhaps the most incredible footage of him that exists. I play an out-of-print VHS copy, always worried about the tape breaking someday. Of course, I choose "The Star Spangled Banner" to illustrate one of the themes of the class—the power of the electric guitar. Most of the students had seen the Woodstock film, but not the solo Hendrix performance. As the close-ups of his huge hands on the white guitar dominate the video screen, I gaze across the room at my students, not knowing any of them.

What do they think of Jimi? Old guitar god? Woodstock as old news? "My parents' music," as some of them claim on their first-day questionnaires? Faces devoid of excitement shine in the dim lights of the room. I want to know what his Banner storm means to them. I ask around the room, but first-day shyness brings only four responses.

"That's one of the most awesome things I've seen," one guy says, "but you don't see it very often. Does his stuff sell?"

"Why did he pick 'The Star Spangled Banner'?" a girl asks in a serious tone.

"I don't know anybody who listens to Jimi Hendrix," another guy states. "But when we hear his stuff, my friends want to know more. He's really not in anymore, though I know lots of people who download his stuff."

"My parents played the Beatles, Bob Dylan, and the Rolling Stones, over and over, when I was a little girl," a fourth student comments. "I think my father thought Hendrix was too loud to play at home."

I move on without telling them that on December 17, 1990, Sotheby's in London auctioned the white Fender Stratocaster that Jimi used to play "The Star Spangled Banner" at Woodstock for $324,000. This buy sent vintage guitar prices skyrocketing into a new era. The anonymous buyer knew the guitar was not in mint condition, the instrument showing scratch marks and cigarette burns. I play "Machine Gun" from the Band of Gypsys DVD, trying to show the students how the news footage from Vietnam and the haunting explosions of Jimi's guitar fit into what is going on in Iraq today, how politics and music will be a major topic for the course. Again, few of them respond, though they stare at the screen as American bombers drop their payloads on the Vietnamese countryside and wounded GIs are carried away in stretchers, the devastating feedback from Jimi's guitar shooting down all pretense that the music was for a distant time in the past.

> It's best to have violence on stage and watch it on TV than do it yourself.
> —Jimi Hendrix on the "Star Spangled Banner"

On the last day of class, I go in reverse and return to the Monterey Pop Festival. I play "Wild Child" as the last video clip for the semester. The whirlwind of electric air and Jimi twisting his guitar begin the song, the young musician so alive and energetic compared to later appearances in his career. My favorite part of his performance is not the guitar burning, but the way he snaps his bubble gum at the end of the line, "Wild Child. You move me!" Pop. The class period is over halfway through the song, so some of the schedule-conscious students start to leave the room as Jimi smashes his guitar against the amplifiers, humping the equipment in rapid body thrusts. Only four or five students witness the act of Jimi dropping his guitar on the stage and bowing before it as he pulls the bottle of lighter fluid out of his flowered shirt. He throws a match on it as Mitch Mitchell keeps up a rapid, heavy drumming behind him. Jimi calls the gods in a quick prayer with his hands, waving his fingers above the flames. They rise higher, and the ignited guitar seems to be playing on its own, the fire reaching the controls and emitting a tremendous shriek from the amplifiers. Jimi leaps up, grabs the burning guitar, and swings it against the amplifiers. The crowd is screaming and cheering, though the camera captures several shocked faces staring at the ceremony they have just witnessed. Jimi staggers off stage, totally exhausted, and witnesses claim he fell into Brian Jones's waiting arms.

End of song. End of image and concert, the footage of this performance out of print for about thirty years, until DVD technology brought the fire back. The last student to leave my class turns to me as I switch off the DVD. "I wonder what happened to that burned guitar?" he says to me, then walks out.

My latest Hendrix buys take me back to the days of my rare 45 of "51st Anniversary." The two new purchases are *Jimi Plays Berkeley* on DVD, released after several decades of being out of print, and a two-disc set containing Jimi at Woodstock, finally available on DVD, accompanied by *Smash Hits* on CD. Though I have wanted *Jimi Plays Berkeley* for years, numerous screenings of it convince me it is not a good film or a great performance, a conclusion I reach with disappointment and surprise, though the DVD is worth buying for the accompanying audio-only, previously unreleased, second-night concert. Berkeley was a post-Woodstock performance, and Jimi was on the way down, wasted and sullen, barely into the music, though occasional moments of energy shine on "I Don't Live Today" and "Voodoo Child (Slight Return)."

I no longer have to worry about breaking my VHS copy of Jimi at

Woodstock. The DVD version is spectacular. Watching it makes me lose sleep and increases my heart rate for several hours. Next time I teach my rock class, I swear I will play the entire thing. I still want to know what Jimi's recent emergence into the visual power of popular music means to younger generations. What is DVD access doing for his legacy? Yet as I plan my syllabus for the next round, I wonder why I want to know what he means to them. Perhaps only Hendrix fans in their fifties, daydreaming about old 45s from their youth, have noticed how available his music has become. It is as if my little vinyl record of "51st Anniversary" has come back to life by its creator's being so alive these days. Maybe I am wasting my time exposing my students to so much Hendrix; they have their own heroes, starting with Kurt Cobain (another left-handed guitarist who died young) and including the Clash, the Replacements, and the White Stripes. If Jimi remains one of the most innovative and influential guitarists of all time, his sound thunders among them. And it spins through the decades of my now-fantasy search for that tiny black 45 of "51st Anniversary."

The *Smash Hits* CD that comes with the *Woodstock* DVD is the American version because "51st Anniversary" is not on it, though I have a vinyl copy of the British import *Smash Hits* that does. I must have bought the import vinyl more than thirty years ago, and it was the first time I had reacquired "51st Anniversary" since my 45 went missing. I also have the remastered CD of the Jimi Hendrix Experience's first album, *Are You Experienced?* containing the original British lineup with "51st Anniversary" on it. Again, it is a song left off the original 1967 American vinyl release of the album, my copy standing in the midst of my ancient vinyl collection, the cardboard cover wearing off. I play "51st Anniversary" from the *Are You Experienced?* CD and recall that Jimi once said in an interview that the obscure song was about his parents, specifically his mother, who died when he was only ten years old. His late father was chiefly responsible for continuing his legacy and seeing that historic footage made it onto DVDs. I play the song a second time and picture the tiny closet in my bedroom in my mother's house where I used to stack my records. On a visit home last year, I walked through my old room and noticed the closet next to the wall where the old desk used to sit. The stage for my air guitar days was long gone. I stood there for a moment, then slid the door open. The closet that once held hundreds of vinyl albums and 45s was dark and empty.

I traveled inside my grandmother Julia's ear and forgot how to wish her good-bye when she died at age ninety-six. I was too far into her ear canal to recognize she was gone. Before I knew it, I had to escape her death by sleeping for three weeks, then waking to one of the heaviest rainstorms I had seen in years. By then, her funeral had taken place, and I walked home alone, afraid I was still counting nightmares from some forgotten childhood encounter with an underwear thief.

I traveled inside my broken thumb, running away from the playground bullies in time to get hit by a speeding train that made the news without killing me. I was too deep into my fear to feel the pain, so it took three months to recover. They never found my left leg, though there was a prayer in my grandmother's Bible about God and the left feet of running men. By the time I got to the great book, I had changed and was released in time for my first lesson in a second language—cabezonmadrelustredilantosytolmustiquilla.

I traveled behind the mule and laughed at my situation because my mother's family had fled their farms at the start of the revolution, abandoning the land to the troops that surrounded my grandmother when she was eleven years old. When her older brother hid behind a pile of donkey shit, he survived the massacre and fled north with his sister. By then, I was a hair on my grandmother's head, the follicle crossing the border illegally, the smell of flowers and soap washing me the day she met my grandfather at the age of fourteen, the young couple kissing under the first cottonwood that would rain its white seeds on their heads.

My mother was obsessed with making sure I grew up with normal feet. She took me to the foot doctor when I was seven years old, and he told her I had flat feet from the extra weight I carried. She was distraught because no son of hers could have abnormal feet, the doctor adding that my feet might grow inward like a chimpanzee's. In 1959, preventive cures for my kind of foot problems were extreme. The doctor measured my arches and toes, their width and length, twisting my ankles with his cold hands until they hurt. He stood me in a pan of liquid resembling green Jell-o, a casting substance for correcting my missteps.

We returned to the doctor the next day, and he appeared in the crowded waiting room with two gruesome-looking things—transparent green molds of the bottom of my feet, the green liquid having dried into special arches I had to wear inside my shoes. He presented the ugly things in front of waiting patients, made me take off my shoes, and inserted the green plastic inside. When I stepped into them, the hard arches pressed painfully into the bottom of my feet. I had to walk in them wherever I went, my days at school filled with excruciating pressure inside my shoes, my classmates teasing me as the new cripple who couldn't take a normal step. I came home one day and had a fit, crying to my mother that I would not wear the arches as I threw one against the wall. It shattered into sparkling pieces of green, and I never wore them again. They were eventually replaced by "corrective" shoes that would have fit Frankenstein, thick soles and a tight space for my feet the latest version of discomfort.

My mother's struggle to correct my feet went on for several months. When it was clear that devices of torture were not working on my abnormal feet, she came upon a new strategy. In the late 1950s, diet pills were the latest medical breakthrough, and she found a doctor who prescribed them to me. They came in a square white box, like a pack of cigarettes, and looked like brown M&M candies. One week after I began taking them, my legs swelled like balloons, a painful rash broke out over my body, and I lost the ability to walk. I couldn't even stand up and so lay in bed with a high fever until I was rushed to the hospital. I spent one week in intensive care, missing school for two weeks before returning to class with flat feet and no weight loss. My humiliation was complete, my silence in public perhaps molded in that year of green arches and brown diet pills.

Forty-eight years later I still have flat feet and recently saw a cousin of mine who had suffered worse in those years of medical experimentation to correct deep family fears of boys with abnormal feet. Ten years younger, Manny was born with his feet grown inward, the bone above the ankles twisting them toward each other. As a baby, he went through several operations to correct the problem, including intentional breaking of the leg bones to reset them correctly! As a boy, he walked on his toes, unable to set his heels down, his feet still bent inward. He eventually outgrew the problem and was a star athlete in high school. When I saw him at a family funeral, he walked like a normal young man. What my mother feared for her son happened to others, and they suffered for years. What my mother tried to do for my feet corrected my naive notions of the world. If you hurt, your peers would take advantage and laugh at you. If you were being molded to exist in a different body, life-threatening experimentation was part of the formula for erasing family abnormalities.

About one year after I broke the green arch on the wall, I was rummaging through my box of plastic toy soldiers, grabbing handfuls to set up a mock battle on the floor. My hand scraped the bottom of the cardboard box in search of one of my favorite soldiers. Instead of miniature helmets and guns, I felt smooth plastic and pulled the surviving green arch out of the box. I have no idea why anyone would drop it in my toys. I certainly didn't put it there, though I found it useful. I made a boat out of it, placed it on the floor as an invasion craft for my favorite army, and set a squad of riflemen on it to hit the beach and conquer the other side.

Part Two

The Arches

I have spent the second part of my life breaking the stones, drilling the walls, smashing the doors, removing the obstacles I placed between the light and myself.

—Octavio Paz, *Eagle or Sun?*

I step under the cracking stone arch and emerge into an abandoned patio and garden. Dying plants and low bushes dry and wither in the immense heat that covers the courtyard, its bricks bleached white from the relentless sheet of light that has led me to enter the abandoned hacienda. There is no one around, this former winery and private home standing empty for years, its last owner dying of cancer. It is located a few miles south of Chamberino, New Mexico, in the Mesilla Valley. Another winery thrives a few miles north of here as this place slowly crumbles into the earth, serving as a memorable icon of poetic openings where I saw something thirty years ago. I walk under the arch leading into the courtyard, its worn bricks curving geometrically under the yellow sky. The open passage has rejected decades of vines, dust, and the occasional lizard and snake that have crawled up its finely matched stones, its tight, disintegrating slabs of architecture allowing me to pass underneath. It was here, in the early 1970s, where a long-lost friend brought me and showed me the one-story white house, a hacienda he claimed was as mysterious as our first attempts to become poets and to articulate the process in our conversations. We were careful as we explored its outer walls and took a peek through its multiple glass windows. I was in my midtwenties, and I believed anything he wanted me to believe about poetry. Our friendship would be the one to disappear as he vanished from the university one semester, but not before showing me this long house he had found on one of his lone treks into the valley.

I stand in the empty courtyard, but can't remember much about the history of the structure. A winery sign hung for years by the front stone wall, the long house set back about one hundred yards from the highway, acres of unused cotton and chili fields surrounding it on three sides. I move toward the main doors of the house and stop before an intricate maze of vines and branches from surviving mimosa and salt cedar trees that cover the front wall. Piles of dry bushes and tumbleweeds are stacked against the stone fence that encloses the courtyard. An old picnic table with a couple of its top beams broken lies on its side near the front door. It is easy to peer inside the windows that line the front room, one whole wall nothing but glass, dozens of panes frozen in a cloudy film that allows partial light in between random streaks of white paint someone sprayed on the glass, as if camouflaging the panes might keep things inside the house from being seen. I trip over a bundle of wire protruding in the debris and almost lose my balance, but manage to land upright by the doors. I look around to see if anyone witnessed my awkward approach. There is no one there. The tall, wooden doors are bolted shut, and iron bars are locked over them. I kick a tumbleweed aside and shade my eyes with my hand as I stick my face near the glass. After wiping dust and dry mud off one of the square panes, I manage to get a foggy view of the empty room inside. The rectangular space disappears in dusty shadows, many of the floorboards sinking into the ground. About a dozen crates and several stacks of wooden poles lie broken and scattered across the room.

Then I see it. It is still there. After three decades and years of rare thoughts about the hacienda, the object of my visit hangs on the far wall. I rub more dirt off the glass and press my face into the glass that reflects the heat of the day. Careful not to burn myself, I squint, then stare into the stationary darkness to locate it again. Its shape, the form of memory and the geometric uncovering that has repelled time, is contained on that wall. The interior of the house is nothing but white walls, room after room of exposed white barriers, invisible white doorways—possible white movements inside an imprisoned space. I keep staring, and, despite the world of white, the thing I want to focus on is on the left wall, near an arch that rises, bends, and explodes into an interior I cannot enter.

When I fell as a boy, I flew under the arch of the kitchen doorway in my grandmother's house and landed against the ticking stove, my head hitting it and knocking me out. It was only the latest episode of my losing consciousness because the door jams in every room of her house rose one inch off the floor, high enough for me to trip about once every couple of weeks, my silly wanderings through rooms laden with the aroma of fresh beans and tortillas frozen in time after my running into a room and tripping. My loss of the real world lasted only a few minutes as the old woman picked me up in her arms and gently carried me to the sofa or bedroom, patiently bringing me back to life. I do not know how she woke me, what she used to bring me back to consciousness. I can't remember the shock of smelling salts or herbal mixtures she used to rub on my aching arms and legs when I complained about my pains. I never asked Julia what she did to make me wake up, perhaps because the first thing I would see each time I opened my eyes after a fall was a cracked arch that marked an entrance into the many rooms of her house—peeling architecture from a childhood that contained a great amount of solitude, my mental explorations and early attempts to write often coming after simply staring at the walls of my grandmother's house, sitting in some dark corner in an overstuffed chair and staring at walls, corners, doors, and arches that would arc toward hallways and barriers that I often refused to explore, one of the reasons for my hesitation lying in the fact that I had started noticing the heavy crucifixes of Christ that hung on several walls in the house. I did not really know what they meant, even if I imitated my parents and grandmother by making the sign of the cross across my shoulders sometimes. I was too young to have faith clearly passed on from parents who rarely went to church. It was up to the old woman, but she frightened me with her mute prayers, her rosaries, and those metal and wooden crosses mounted everywhere.

After bringing me back from my falls, my grandmother would leave me lying alone for a few minutes. My eyes would flutter open to greet ceilings and perfectly designed arches that contained a house full of life, while at the same time their shapes extended toward corners and shadows where a grandmother silently refused to give up many of her magical secrets. Both of my parents worked all day, so the vibrant movement that accented the hours took place between a busy elderly person laboring to keep a huge house clean and perfect and a boy discovering the awe of quiet and solitude by staring at walls and arches. When I fell as a boy, I retreated into a momentary space that pulled me back into unknown origins of ancestral time that probably formed my need to create. I did not know that losing consciousness here and there was an early stage of sleeping and reawakening. These states, brought about by running and falling, would lead me to thrive in the deep shell of a house that eventually granted me the gift of writing by unleashing an imagination that seeded itself in those rooms with their high arches, the constant smell of fresh Mexican food mixing with invisible motions my grandmother waved over me to wake me up. Never mind that doctors later found I was passing out because I was anemic—I decided, early on, that I fell and blacked out as a small boy because it was a rite of passage from infancy to a beginning awareness of the world around me. This existence began with an old woman taking care of me as part of the process of letting go in order to embrace my imagination. I recounted this idea to a writer friend decades later, and he cried, "Robert Desnos! Robert Desnos!" I didn't know who Desnos was until my friend told about the famous surrealist poet of the early twentieth century who spontaneously fell into dream states in the middle of conversations and began to recite poems he created on the spot. He sometimes woke on his own. At other times, his exasperated friends would wake him and force him to write down what he had echoed in his trances. I laughed when my friend tried to compare me to Desnos because I couldn't write in childhood, though, again, each time I awoke from these blackouts, it was the image of arches that met me first. When my eyes opened and I was OK, it was that geometric bending and solid dimensions on the walls of my grandmother's house that took me away, day by day, month by month, until I began to see past the arches and walls and rooms. Then, as I got older, perhaps five or six years old, I quit having these fainting spells. By then, I had already acquired the habit of sitting in the den of the house to follow the solid bend of arches over the doorway, their careful arc holding up the old walls. I wondered how they were shaped, and as a child I suspected that those contained spaces were constructed so I could wake up, sit up, take a deep breath, and put my tiny shoes back on. Then I would take off again, running through the clean hallways of a waiting house whose geometric unfoldings were opening to let me pass through.

Staring at the white wall inside the hacienda makes me tap the window gently, then knock the glass hard. Without breaking it, I tap again and gaze inside at what I came to see. The black outline of a crucifix lives on the wall, its fading cross perfect in its survival during my years of being gone from the Southwest, absent from an area bought and sold, renovated and reformed to make room for hundreds of thousands of people who have moved to the region since I left, though not a single one of them has entered here to erase the cross. The silhouette of the crucifix stays on the wall because vast changes across the desert have not yet reached these walls. I want to breathe a sigh of relief, but it is not inside me. I have been gone too long. Yet the decades cannot remove the need to come here and find it so easily. I take another look. Whatever heavy crucifix hung there, years ago, is gone. Its shadow remains petrified onto the white fields of enclosure and divorce—that separation between private worship and public ceremony. Through the dirty window glass, I can barely trace the remaining lines that look like ash or chalk, as if someone intentionally took a marker and traced the outline of the crucifix before taking it away as part of abandoning the place. This dwelling was never a church, but a site for someone's desire to symbolize his faith, following it until it led to this immense space whose walls needed to be marked with a universal sign that gave identity to the household. The cross must have been at least three feet long with the arms extending one foot on each side. I study the image and accidentally press my right cheek to the glass, the hot surface stinging and making me bounce back. I rub my cheek and try again. It is definitely a cross, the mark of an old crucifix from a holy mounting emblazoned into the materials that have kept the magnificent hacienda looking like it was a wonderful place to have lived. Its history of ownership is locked in some country clerk's office, though it is displayed here on a public level if anyone bothers to walk up, as I did. How has this negative of a cross survived all these years? Was the actual cross on the wall when my long-lost friend brought me here long ago? I can't remember.

I move quickly to another spot along the rows of windows and have to climb over empty wooden crates thrown against the house, some broken, others serving as frames for the intricate webs and tightly wound nests of the many black widows I spot and am careful to avoid as I move along the cracked adobe walls that face the north side of the house. The windows extend the entire length of the wall. I try to imagine what it must have been like to enjoy sitting in a such a sunny room during a cool fall day, the writing table waiting for a moment when memory can't carry itself any longer and something must be set down to find a way into the implosion of rooms beyond the windowed corridor—the basic discipline of needing to pass under arches a practice of the solitary occupant of this enormous and self-contained house.

From my new angle, I can see clearly through the glass. The burned intaglio of the cross is real and defies the age and decay before me. It is not a miracle, but a remnant of the past when grapes on the vine must have covered this place, the huge outline of the cross keeping the meaning of its role here a secret. It is gone as everything here is vanished, though the arches into other rooms, suddenly illuminated by my shift in location, prove nothing has been abandoned. Instead, it has stopped in time. I have been gone from my homeland for twenty-eight years now, half of my life. My origins of being, staying, and leaving are imprisoned in houses like this one—dwellings, barrios, and adobe shelters guarded by arches that propel invisible equations upon the visitor and upon the one who originally constructed their bending forms. The black outline of a cross, whether intaglio or pictograph, is merely the sign of needing to forget and move on. I will say it again. The mysterious lines on the white walls I first saw decades ago have not faded or been defaced by anyone breaking into a place abandoned for a very long time. No one has bothered to whitewash or paint over the shadow, allowing the burning symbol to join the white possibilities in the other rooms. The actual cross that originally hung on that wall for years was the only thing that needed to be taken. The rest of the enclosed world, within my memory of tripping and passing out as a child and within these trapped arches, remains. Whoever owned this hacienda cleared out a long time ago, and the heavy crucifix was valuable to this person, though I can't understand how a hanging object could push or make an impression on the wall. It isn't dust or the grime of years. It is an eternal sign. Its weight and density would pull it down, toward the floor, not against the plaster.

I feel the heat of the day on the glass as I blink, the sweat starting to run down my forehead as I want to cover every detail—someone painted the cross on there. No. It is an impression, a clue, a pressing against the wall to the left of the arch that leads away, the same process as my grandmother's pressing rose petals flat into her Bible—a similar transformation that pressed other rose petals into deep red beads on a rosary she gave me years before she died, the ever-present aroma of roses encased in the tiny plastic box where she kept it. I blink as the sweat stings my eyes. Pulling back from the window, I hear a dog bark in the distance and wonder if someone is approaching from the highway. I turn to my left, but do not spot any cars pulling in next to mine, the huge cottonwood shading the vehicle from the 100-degree heat. As I turn back to the glass, something moves inside the room.

In a white room that descends into memory and gives language permission to enter the heart and the mind, despite the desert heat and the awareness that home is a punishing force that can kill the fuse, the meter and the source of understanding originate. This is the will to keep passing through arches that extended their curved design toward opposite levels of experience and doubt, the space for passing and entering existing to give speech a chance to marry its silence with the infinite designs of stone and mortar—the way to extracting and writing first poems. The house falls down, and the speaker steps out of it through surviving frames and arches above doors that refuse to open or close—dimensions found in the poetic shape of the mind that rose from ancient beds and sofas in childhood houses, passing through the corridors of memory to leave the house. This departure comes when the arches of time have done their duty by simply standing there, structured and muscled, carved and designed to shelter and hide, cover and maintain, as they keep things inside, the few inhabitants who leave the house, forever, having to gaze elsewhere because the desert sky often refuses to bridge its thin layers of clouds together, preferring the wide-open canyon of blue that cannot be breached by the lines of remembering, the cracked rainbows of brick and mortar.

The lizard is jealous of its shadow and keeps chasing it under the rocks. The hot wind is afraid of its own brightness and sweeps the dust clouds through the canyon. The dry riverbed points south, but the washed sand swirls north, the brown waves creating more shadows the lizard can't overcome. The lizard is jealous of its shadow, and it is starting to disappear, the last marks in the sand are the patterns it created when the river threw it back and released the migrant-worker huts upon dry land.

The reptile is tasting itself, weaving its blue tail into its red mouth, the circle created when it runs out of breath, and the dark patterns in the sky keep falling ahead of its tracks, the rolling creature of light setting the storm on fire, igniting any last clue as to why it is envious of its own gain, the way it migrates past the mountains to take its place among the alphabets, the scattered stones, the shattered arches that once spelled a path where no being would be afraid.

After having to bend to pass under the low arch, I grab a fistful of dirt from the hole in the floor and put it into a plastic bag. There are few choices for redemption or salvation above the cold floor of desire, grains of this holy dirt sprinkled on the concrete as if timeless pairs of hands have been carelessly dropping the dirt on the way out of the sanctuary. What falls here can never be regathered. Miracles are dug out of the ground, and the benefits are strung throughout the room—thousands of tiny *milagros* petrified into the silence of worship. Miniature legs, hands, feet, crutches, human figures. Photos of ill children, husbands and wives, parents and teenagers shot in gang warfare. One haunting display of portraits of two Chimayo policemen killed during a drug bust in the early 1980s. Prayers for the dead, the dying, and the ones who make it back, most of the items accompanied by slips of paper left there by relatives seeking a cure and a moment, a sign from their Lord that the power of the bare ground means there is a power above it waiting to heal. I read a few. "Dear Jesus, Please help Rolando. He is in the hospital with cancer." "I will do two novenas for my Gloria. She is missing two years. Please find her." "Thank you, God. My Marta is no longer sick." The roll call of pain. The echoes of thanks. Hundreds of slips and names and notes to fill a book of the dead and a book of the living. The book of thousands who have entered this room to take a handful of dirt.

I wonder how many survive, their return to life a temporary ritual before the final burial, the silenced prayers finding a spot in this crowded room of eternal thanks. Yet the walls are also lined with generations of people who did not respond to prayers and did not get well after the novenas. I always thought milagros were only for those who benefited from the healing power of their God. As I stroll around the small chamber on the left side of the sanctuary, I see that those whose prayers were answered are mixed with the unchosen. Promises kept and promises ignored by the healing dirt that has come out of the hole for hundreds of years. Believers say it is the sand of testament and ritual that is never empty, the hole mysteriously replenished of its dirt.

I put my bag of sand in my pocket and stare down at the opening in the earth. A bottomless chanting to heal the sick and the crippled, the addicted and the blind. The dozens of saints on the walls look at me in silent grace, their portraits reminding me of my grandmother's walls of calendar saints. A bottomless memory of asking for too many things from hidden belief, though faith is illuminated on every ancient and recent image of a saint displayed here. San Antonio, San Cristóbal, San Martín, San Ignacio, San José, and every icon of men and women I can't name. A bottomless well of hope.

I stare at the hole, then look behind me because I feel someone entering the room. Several low voices echo across the empty sanctuary and old pews, a few candles by the altar glowing across the interior darkness of the church. Four people kneel in different rows, their heads bowed. Am I hearing their prayers? I look at the hole again and think of a kiva. Two days ago I visited Indian ruins nearby and saw the enormous opening in the ground, its circular walls lined in red stone, a *No Trespassing* sign keeping me out of the ceremonial chamber that native people had dug out of the desert. A kiva. A church with a hole full of dirt that never runs out. A reaching down into what lies below the surface, these extending acts stretching into an interior away from low and high arches that decide other things. It is not the sun or the heavens of yearning that spread above the arches, but a direction down, perhaps to a place where belief begins. Kiva and church sinking, their milagros and artifacts going into the soil after walls can no longer hold up the chants. Kiva and church bringing worshippers closer to earth gods who were hiding underground for millennia, the fact that this famous hole at Chimayo never runs out of dirt a sign that perhaps those gods have been digging their way out as their believers have been digging down.

I start to leave, having to bend down again to clear the arch of the low entrance into the room of dirt. The voices in the sanctuary stop. As I turn to gaze at the abundance of mementos and photographs one last time, I hear the tinkling of bells and smell incense, make sure my bag of dirt is stuffed into my pocket as I leave the church. I emerge into the blazing New Mexico evening whose fiery sky paints the valleys and arroyos red before their terrain is washed by a river searching for a new entrance into the earth.

The black lines on the wall do not let me into the hacienda, and I do not try. I stare through the glass because I saw something move inside, a brief blurring of image and shadow down one of the hallways I can barely make out from where I stand. I assume rats, bats, and other creatures of the desert have loved this place for a long time. I saw something move, and it was much larger, darker, and it disappeared in the back of the house. An intruder? I guess I am the intruder, and I am not afraid, though I glance at my watch and wonder if it is time I leave for good. I keep my face close to the window, the sweat pouring down into my eyes. As I wipe it away, I move a couple of feet to my left and cannot see the outline of the cross any longer. It is best because I think of my lost poet friend Gary and wonder what happened to him. We stood near this same spot and fantasized about buying the place and starting a writers' retreat. Nice dream because he was gone from the writing program only a few months later. Nice dream because we stared at the shadow of the cross on the wall and agreed we were "recovering Catholics," the need to be poets taking us farther away from our upbringing. So what if we came across the weird mark on the wall that clearly showed someone had hung a huge cross there for a very long time? He or she was gone, the place boarded up, and any ghostly remains of a faith we had questioned were best left imprisoned inside. I think I told my mother, a strict Catholic, about what I saw, and she told me that old crucifixes, especially those made of certain metals, could easily rust in their own way and leave marks on the wall. I suggested we drive in the Mesilla Valley one weekend so I could show her the hacienda, but she refused, claiming that such signs could also be the markings of something dangerous, unexplained—a warning that could only be mounted and trapped under eternal arches that bent their mysteries from one arc to the other. Perhaps there were too many rooms to tear down, too many other signs inside that I could not discover; as I moved farther down the wall, I came to the front door and rattled the lock on the bars.

I dreamed of ancient houses the other night. No one wanted to hear about it. I dreamed of old hallways where no one woke up and no one spoke. I was there and dwelled in the dark corner of a cold adobe wall. No one said it was beautiful. I was there and opened one window because no one stayed in the house of my dreams. Evacuation took place long ago, and I dreamed I was the only one who stayed. No one let me knock on the door, and I simply would not open it without permission. I dreamed of ancient houses without doors, where no one left and no one entered. I saw a black hallway, and I could not move. No one turned the corner or got in my way. I saw another empty room and paused. No one was there, and no one called as I kept dreaming of ancient houses that survived the fire that no one started and nobody put out. The smoke was in the walls. Perhaps that is why the cross came through it. I was there to trace the smell of smoke in the dry mud. All I had to do was press my nose against the cold wall.

No one claimed the houses or the streets surrounding the dwelling of my dream. I kept dreaming that I was standing on a stone porch. No one passed, and no animal dwelled there. I was the only one waiting for the morning, and I waited there still, steam rising from the clay cup of coffee I found on the blackened stove in the empty kitchen of an abandoned house. No one woke while I drank it, and no one slept because I was the one dreaming of ancient houses the other night.

One of the last things my grandmother told me before her final years were lost in senility and the inability to recognize anyone who sat by her bed was a story she called "The Mud Man." Ninety-six-year-old Julia tried to sit up against the pillows and face the chair where I sat at her side, extending a cold, bony hand to me.

The mud man came out of the Rio Grande the night before my grandfather Bonifacio died. He was a secret thought in the village—a mud man covered in the slime of slaves. Body of brown crosses and startled hair. Body of stinking clay and leaves in the eyes.

The mud man danced on the far bank of the river, cottonwood limbs moving above his head. He was blind and crusted into the brain. Unable to talk, he wandered the upper valley, frightened the crows, and lit fires with his feet. In one house, my grandfather lay dying, the smell of approaching mud keeping him alive. When the candles around his bed went out, he raised one hand and pointed to the door. My grandmother opened it in silence. The mud man stood there dripping his life. When the mud man approached, my grandfather closed his eyes. The last thing my grandmother recalled was her husband's mask coming off, the bright streaks of mud across his face showing her what he looked like as a boy. The mud man flew out through the window as my grandmother shouted a curse at the fleeing form of her husband. Family members arrived, though they refused to pass under the arch of the front door into fresh death. When they saw the mud, they said a prayer or two because when the river floods, there is no mud man. When the river dries, the mud man might come, but no one has seen him since the death of my grandfather and no one says anything about the mud on the shoes of every man who survived his death.

A man walks into a church and finds he is the only person in the dark sanctuary. He goes to the altar where several votive candles are quietly burning. He stops in front of a peeling statue of la Virgen de Guadalupe, bows down before the shrine, and makes the sign of the cross. A bat suddenly flies out of nowhere and streaks across the chamber. Startled, he follows the darting creature with his eyes as it disappears beyond the choir balcony. He turns back to the candles so he can pray, but is disrupted by a drop of water landing on his sleeve. He looks up at the distant ceiling in time for a second drop to hit him on the chin. It's raining outside, and the roof is leaking. The man moves on his knees a couple of feet down the bench and begins his first Our Father. He is halfway through the prayer when an altar boy, mumbling incoherently, runs from the priest's chamber, his footsteps echoing through the church. The man is distracted again as the boy, dressed in his colorful frock, takes one of the small burning candles and returns to the back room. The man shakes his head at the trail of wax the boy drips on the floor. This time he manages a complete Our Father and two Hail Marys before a dense cloud of incense fills the air around the statue. He begins to cough, and his eyes start to burn. He rises to his feet and notices that the poison sweetness of the incense is coming from the priest's chamber. He coughs and walks back there, but the incense makes him nauseous, and he stops at the door. Inside, the altar boy is holding the ugly bat over the candle flame, its wings folded so it won't escape. Next to him, an old priest is crying and shaking his head, his clothes soaked from the rain, a pot of incense hanging from a rope in his outstretched hand. The man turns and bolts down the long aisle between the pews. As he reaches the sanctuary doors, he spots the containers of holy water mounted on the walls. He can't resist and dips a finger in one of them, then raises the wet finger to trace a cross on his forehead. This act sets off a loud clattering of wings behind him, but he does not turn to look. When he opens the door, it is early evening, and the rain has stopped, everything under the sky wet and shiny. Hundreds of bats pour out of an open window below the bell tower. They fill the sky as the man stands under the arch, not quite sure where he parked his car. Three more altar boys come up the concrete stairs toward him, and he gets out of the way as two priests embrace each other on the sidewalk near the street.

I pull on the heavily bolted doors like a fool. The lock and bars rattle in my hands, the ancient wood on the other side actually creaking as if the door is going to break open. Maybe the doors are old and weak, time making the locks and bars ineffective. I take both hands and pull and pull, hoping something will give way as my T-shirt is sprinkled with my flying sweat.

Snapping branches and something heavy hitting the ground behind me make me stop. Startled, I spin around to be met by an empty courtyard, the front gate open, my car parked quietly, and a steady hot wind moving through the cottonwoods. I cross the front bricks that line the porch and think I hear something rustling behind the huge mound of tumbleweeds trapped against the right adobe wall. It could be a rattlesnake or a lizard. I pick up a small rock from the ground and toss it into the weeds. Nothing.

I move closer to the weeds when I spot something white entangled among the dry, twisted branches of the yellow and brown weeds. It is an old newspaper, a torn sheet from the *El Paso Times*. I pull it off and see it is a page from the Sunday "Religion" section, the newsprint smeared, the yellow sheet smelling old. I roll it into a ball with both hands and toss it over the wall. As I turn toward the front door again, I spot a tiny red-and-blue square on the ground. I reach down and pick up a plastic novena card. It is a laminated photograph of la Virgen de Guadalupe, a Catholic prayer in Spanish printed in gold ink on the other side. I stop myself from throwing it over the wall and tuck it into my pants pocket instead.

Visiting the area, I always stay at my mother's house, the home of my youth after we moved from my grandmother's house. My mother's place is "newer," built with colorful rooms and modern doorways whose vertical rectangles would never allow the idea of an arch. I stay there in the heat and dream that after the river fell, fathers and mothers came out of the mud. I stayed to watch them rise, trusting that the dawn is measured by how we love and love again. Deranged rattlesnake humming for sanctuary, tracing patterns in a sand disintegrating toward my new skin. I woke in the fire house, emerged as a blackened fish painted on the stone jar dripping its thirst down my hands that held it as I took a drink. I woke as the pictograph, a symbol missing both feet, my wings outlawed by a sweet bird that descended to drink from the stone jar first.

On this site in 1532, near the hacienda I have returned to, Alonso Martínez de Salinas withdrew his sword from the saguaro and gasped at the stream of flying spiders that poured out of the tall, thick cactus. The spiders bounced off his steaming armor, and Alonso stood there, hoping the current of awful things would stop emerging into the air. On this spot, he knelt and prayed for his wife and son, whom he had not seen in twelve years, since his journey in search of gold and truth had taken him into the land of amputated people, groups of them asking him to give up his collection of their arms, feet, and legs. On this rock in the same year, Alonso saw his first angel and proceeded to swing at it with his sword, his horse spooked by the fluttering wings, the rest of his men lost in the canyons for days. When he tired of stabbing at the night, Alonso paused at the edge of the cliff and watched a burning object cross the magnificent sky in seconds, its bright path realigning the desert stars so Alonso could carve his name and the name of his father on the red rock. I pass the marker on the way to the hacienda and can't help but stop and read what it says. On this site in 1956, a marble slab was erected by the state to give viewers the truth about conquest and the preserved alphabet of the lost, slashing lines of heavenly swords that cut the saguaro open each time a traveler stops and notices the dripping of sap on the ancient plant.

> The sun isn't leaving. It is still stubbornly insisting on staying in the room. What time is it? One numeral more or one less moves my hours, the hour of my definite loss.
> —Octavio Paz, *Eagle or Sun?*

The front door to my mother's house is falling apart. I don't know why she has not replaced the original double doors of a forty-year-old house with more secure doors. They have locks, but you can shake the doors when they are locked, and they are loose in their frames, ready to come off. I have been going in and out of those doors for those forty years, and the colors of the wood on the opening have changed during that time. Pink or blue or green or a dark brown. Currently, they are blue, the color of prosperity and warmth and the nest of time and welcome. Of course, as tall, rectangular doors, they do not sit under a curved arch, but in the plane of entrance and exit—measured limits of what was possible and what never happened, corners and turns that mark the changing patterns of family, the runaway father and husband passing under the straight arch to flee the family so he can enter other houses, other nests whose twisted legs and arms have fallen beneath the arches of a border darkness that will not explain itself to anyone.

I enter on a recent visit and stand in the foyer, wondering how the rooms have changed since my last visit. I hold the door open as if someone else is coming in behind me, but I am alone. My mother greets me, and the house is quiet, the front hallway turning sharply to the right, pointing at angles that reveal a farther door, a shudder and a step inside a glass eye where we love what we love, don't even hold it in our arms. I enter her house and shake my head at the feeble door, knowing that for every sight like this, there is a movement—the shadow we kiss before we get old like this woman. For every object we touch or every door we knock on, a touching back—the fingerprints remaining years after we leave to go be someone else. A door, a shoulder, a photograph we didn't know we were in—blackened trees swaying about our heads, the frame capturing the lightning strike behind the house. For every recognition, a room behind stamina unseen by what we wanted. For every love, a whispering to flee and to know that for each birth there is a false idol sitting on a high shelf near a window or an exit, someone calling to us to wait before our trembling hands reach up to touch our faces, but sway and touch the white wall instead.

The lizard arches in the air, the red bubble forming under its chin like a blood bruise that has burst in greeting. It trembles on the pile of bricks and vanishes into the wall. I pause and think I smell shit, perhaps the odor of decay. I step back under the dry mud arch and find the lizard is gone and I am back in the exterior of a place I have wanted to enter for more than half of my life. The hacienda will not let me in because the sign of the cross on its walls is a monument to the possibilities that gospel history must stop, needs to end and have its locked doors blown open by an incredible explosion of heat so that I can see why I keep coming back, why the early youth of poetry is the middle-aged man of doubts and texts, his peering through hot windows merely an act of longing that cannot bring the past into the present because the crucifix that was mounted on the white wall of internal dwelling was hung there as a magnet for the present moment—the force that lights a desert path for those who want to believe the cross comes first, its conquistadors and burning pueblos glowing in the smoke of history, the black marks on white walls allowed to stay by some invisible hammer that pounds those lines back onto the cracking surfaces where no human hands will ever worship again. I rush to the window where I first looked into the room; my breath on the glass is still there, and the far white wall does not move simply because my faith was transformed into the need to write something down, to say farewell to the friend who disappeared in the name of poetry, to wave good-bye to the adventure of uncovering certain barriers whose union with the history of conquest meant that these walls would go up, be a part of a settlement for more than a century before everyone surrendered and took their economy elsewhere. In other words, this old place has been closed and empty for more than thirty years, and no one has moved in or seeded the grapes again or even blessed its dying walls because the desert has spread and developed in a different direction. Parts of its landscape have decayed in a manner that tells me that faith and its truths lie over there—across the Organ Mountains, past the Franklin Mountains that surround El Paso, and up the arches of sand that enclose and fence in *la frontera* where I grew up and that I abandoned because I did not want my grandmother's ancient house or my mother's decaying, modern one to shut their doors, seal their windows, and take down their own crosses before I could get out of the way.

Before my young poet friend disappeared, he told me about the love of the path, sleep sounding like the word is listening in the year of the footstep, history's bullet embedded in the king who waved good-bye after his servants quit believing in him. My friend wrote about how the coat of worry submerged in the arms of the angel who voted for yesterday's barrio to return, dirty streets leading to adobe walls where there are no secrets left, the arrow poised for flight, basket of air resembling the fuse, thin measure of the shelf where the story resides like a jewel, lifted body finding the light, waiting for what happens, grabbed bird tagged as rare, geometric rope translated into desire as metaphor against convicted minutes unfolding the knees, that position judged too alive for the meal given with half an hour to live, what is embedded in the skin unstable as the present war that is destroying everything around us, my friend's version of the text crossing the street, unaware of the political hair, the other side posing as witnesses to the original contractor who first built the arches over the courtyard of this hacienda, people running away from the dry valley as proof that there are names left to be contained, history's update including the tie, gloves, and comb that survived what simply wouldn't go away, the museum of afterbirths really the tomb of what had to be born in order to complete the game and finish placing the bricks in their proper, fitted order.

What's at hand arrives with the figure crossing the street at the end of the century, giving each of us a chance to guess which shelter we will live under, to plan what we will do when the spaceships from Roswell arrive in our area. This must be foolish in revelation, destroyed by the powers hidden in our pockets and shaded by adobe towers, our gloves perfect in the approaching autumn that makes no difference in the southern New Mexico desert. When my first poetry teacher came down the stairs, I paused and learned how to breathe, changed my mind about asking him about what is above us and how what settles there is derived from a wish to be alive when light on the stones stains the lovers, giving them time to face the frost before shooting paradise with a word or two. Dead or alive, our lessons are emblems in our hair, the shadows we left on the school building stairs as six-year-old kids. What must come will shake the house, separate us into thriving families and lost dogs who claim a corner or two before the evictors try again, showing proof we arrived at the wrong party, the mistaken ritual of having to sweep the floors with our own hair, primitive brooms we tied before we left.

When they found us doubting the emptiness of the wind, it was too late to call home, so we acted homeless, recalled the strength we found on the living-room rug, memories unable to define what happened on the floor, how we fell down and stayed there, afraid to raise our heads before the wings quit flashing back and forth, black curtains deciding this was our only home, the cold furniture moving as if someone sat there, keeping track of how slowly we rose, sat up, brushed the dust off our clothes, and asked if the willow in the window was still bent toward the pictures of all the saints on the walls.

I quit trying to break into the hacienda because its arches are moving. They are shimmering in the heat, and I left my canteen in the car. When I go and retrieve it, I lean on the hot driver's door and drink, water pouring down my chest, my head thrown back in time to spot the black dog darting out of a side gate in the courtyard, the animal sprinting across the dry fields toward a distant Mexican man who is waving in my direction. He is calling the dog, a Labrador retriever who doesn't bother to bark or notice me as it flies happily to its owner. How long was the dog in the courtyard and where was it hiding? It must have made the heavy thumping noise I heard earlier, but even the mess of tumbleweeds couldn't have hidden such a large animal. I watch it disappear in the waving horizon and take another drink from the canteen. The top of the hacienda is flat, layers of red roofing stones decorating its edges, many of the stones missing, whole sections of their trim gone from the sides of the building. I put the canteen away and stand under the arch that patterns over the front gate. I intentionally stand under it and feel like getting in my car and driving away. I put my right hand on the lowest arched brick that meets the wall. The white plaster peels off, and red dust from the old brick sprinkles onto my hand. I brush it on my pants and stare at a line of black ants as they move up the wall and disappear into a large crack.

Then I see it. The landscape of entrapment and containment, the architecture of release from home through poetic transformation. I see the arches and walls, the adobe ruins and heat, a desert longing that has taken me in circles, until the poems connect the spheres and I am back under the ancient arches. I look at the abandoned hacienda with its strange black marks on its inside wall, and I see the landscape of vertical passage, as if I were climbing the Organ Mountains, which rise like petrified towers about twenty miles behind me. I stand under the arch and I see it—the vertical lift from the vast desert floor to the architecture of love and longing, the designs and arrows and structures that have come and gone in five hundred years of erecting and destroying, occupying and fleeing—whether ranch or poor migrant hut, pueblo or cathedral, grandmother house or easily accessible mother dwelling. It is all right there—the decaying hacienda stamping its image of past discovery and present confinement into the need to write it down, to feel it, to see it, and to know that history often pauses to allow a different form of escape—a fleeing not from truth or what came before I had any idea what the Southwest was all about, but from what arrived here to burn and kill before rebuilding and forming arches that rainbow from power to weakness, from God to snake, from kiva in the underground to stone church in the heavens of tomorrow.

Adornment of Our Lady at San Jerónimo de Taos Mission, New Mexico, 1776

Under the ancient and tiny arch, there is a gilded cardboard crown with a little silver cross on top. The spirits are pleased there is room for them. A new wig has been provided by Father Olaeta to go along with the gauze headdress on la Virgen. The gauze of truth and time may have been torn off the body of a dead local shaman, but such an act would be blasphemous, though someone insisted it be done to show the spirits that their power was capable of everything. There are also small, silver earrings with drops of paper pearls on little wires, which the Lady wore before, but something changed, though they still hang on her ears. Their companion is a small necklace of blue glass beads, bugle beads, and spangles that Father Claramente put on mother-of-pearl ribbon, and from the necklace hang five ordinary crosses that the Lady had before, though the pattern of their hanging on her statue now casts different shadows than the sanctuary has been accustomed to accepting. There is a silk dress with embroidery of the same colors, wrist bands with cambric ruffles edged in gold. The new Brittany chemise cannot be forgotten, for it adds a strength to the Lady's stillness. For her mantel, a small silk towel with blue and white stripes has been chosen. This was made by a devout person who gave it to Father Claramente, and it was made into a mantel by putting ordinary narrow lace around the cloth. The Lady also has a dress and mantel of black ribbed silk. Toward the neck, she wears two strings of paper pearls. There are six ordinary silver reliquaries and a large one of tin plate. Eight little silver shields are arranged on rosettes of blue and mother-of-pearl ribbon, the shields warning the spirits that there is territory here yet to be taken, though the Lady has defined hers already. There is a rosary of silver filigree, a jet cross set in silver, and sixteen medals arranged around her feet—some signifying the number of children slaughtered by the Spanish soldiers, the number of shamans killed, the total number of war clubs confiscated, the array of deities and corn dolls destroyed, the days of the month when it is best to kill; the symbol of the sun representing the church tower and not the soiled sun the people have been kept from worshipping, the image of a sandaled foot of the Christ and not the dancing circle of men who were imprisoned; the horse, the cow, and the pig, each with its own medal, representing the trees burned down, the Rio Grande changing course before God; and the last four medals representing the four worlds the Lady steps on as she makes her way to her morning bath at the river each day, an act hidden from the world by the belief that this statue will move only the day that the cross completely oversees everything and is able to place distance between its shadows and the reconfigured expanse of the arch above it—stones able to dislodge themselves and carry the past toward reconstructing a place for Our Lady.

> When one door is shut, another one opens.
> —Miguel de Cervantes, Don Quixote

It saw me approach and tried to hide. I entered the great adobe room and knew where to look. The face tried to disappear behind a row of masks on the wall, the one it chose the orange snarl of a wolf that pranced around the room when I walked in. The face could not become the creature, and it moved behind the profile of a sleeping woman—the beauty of her dreams filling the walls with shadows in which to hide. I stood there and, after chasing it for years, wanted the face to show itself, but the mask of the woman would not open its eyes, the face staying there until I poured myself a cup of water from a deep, clay jar on the lone table. The spill forced the face to leap from an old man's death mask alongside the features of a village god who destroyed his town with rage and fear, even the tiny mask of a child, its empty eyes blazing as the face I followed dwelled there and returned everything to childhood. The face at Tula did not appear again, and I waited in that room for days, came and stayed away, the face breathing behind the mask of the child. I have not entered the room in years, but see the face in every boy and girl who walks by me, each young approach taking me back to the moment I thought I had captured the face in a poem—the instant one of the masks tilted on its hook—and I touched and scratched my own face, came closer to the breathing clay, blinked my eyes, and wiped the sweat away.

Nothing was brought to me because I forgot how to ask the sparrow to quit jumping on the courtyard wall. It flew away, and I thought of this—a sacred mark on your forehead is a sign someone forgot to pray. But what is a sacred mark on a wall long after the cross is gone? The ones who worked the fields surrounding the hacienda must have been busy digging for roots, uncovering a pattern of deceit in the way the desert allowed them to live. I had a weeping chair, but it was destroyed by an angry man who took the wood and built a tower instead, its shadow rising across the border to announce this is where it begins, where trees burn to allow the stories of grass to sprout in a mud that doesn't dry, its patterns tramped on by a boy who lost his place to sit.

Nothing was brought to me because I owned the sunlight between the cottonwoods, the trees surrounding this old winery reminding me about the beam of knowledge I stole from an old man who refused to cross the river. When he offered a hand, I took his dagger away, but have not seen it since I started listening to the blinding voice that escaped the trees. I think I gave the dagger to my father one day, a rare gift from a son to a father. When I look for someone to believe me, no one cares because the first appearance of truth is the last road I take each time I stand by the Rio Grande and wish I knew who carved the face I was born with into the oldest cottonwood that keeps blocking my way.

Arch in a group of fallen cottonwoods takes the sun away, and I bend low to pass beneath the lowest, twisted limbs behind the courtyard walls. What if I was mistaken, and the desert floor gave way and the treasures of the earth were exposed? What if my father phoned me instead, his twenty years of exile turning back the clock so we could start over again? What if I could fall and pass out in my grandmother's house as a middle-aged man? Would I finally wake up? What if I told a lie and it happened to be true—those blue trees and giant worms I made up actually crawling in my front yard to make me question myself again? What if I went outside and the sun came out and a beautiful woman on a horse casually rode down the street? What if the comic books I collected as a boy of seven suddenly appeared in a decaying cardboard box and begged, with their yellow pages, to be read again? What if I never asked another question, but simply accepted the black widow in the corner of the room? What if I slowed down and let the butterfly fill the book? What if the black lines outlining a cross were actually a true lament that mourned the past and warned me at the same time? What if the house finally let me in?

What if the dream of my dead grandmother flying through the window to say good-bye to me on the morning she passed away was repeated in my sleep, my window open to the summer wind, the shadows of birth and age reflecting off the passage she took to get from here to there? What if I found the word *calexijorllitapquil* etched on a different wall in the locked place and had no idea what it meant? What if I made it up to get past the hands that always reach out whenever I wish to change history by being allowed to break into the house? What if I found the black rosary the old woman gave me twenty years ago, and the beads were tangled within themselves? What if I entered a church and never came out? What if the plan was clear and more sparrows landed in the trees, several of them releasing their droppings so that they splattered all over the arch in the courtyard?

The tumbleweeds in the courtyard write about themselves, and the spell of silence is broken. The black dog starts an awful barking across the fields, and I think I spot his owner slowly walking toward my car. Suddenly, I am lucky to know that the spell over this place is broken by simply standing back and taking a good look at it, peering at the building without staring at the verified marks on the spot where something used to hang on the wall. I find an old shoe lying among the debris and kick it out of my way.

One of the first poems I wrote after my friend first took me to the hacienda was about Rufino Tamayo, the great twentieth-century Mexican painter. I tried to write a poem in response not only to the magnificent solitude and beauty of the place at the time, but as an attempt to combine the love for the landscape of La Mesilla Valley with the distorted images I found in Tamayo's paintings. I had been introduced to his work the previous year during a small exhibit at the library at UTEP, where I was a graduate student in writing. Tamayo's vision of the earth and its anguished human figures caught in astounding poses and exaggerated colors reminded me of many things I had seen in the desert. One of my favorite paintings is *Hombre cerca de la ventana* (Man Standing near a Window). He completed the painting in 1975, only three years before I first stepped through the arch of the gate leading me into the courtyard of the hacienda.

In the painting, Tamayo uses different hues of red and brown that lift off the desert floor to create a robotic-like figure, a man with a square head opening his mouth as if shouting something toward the corner of a red wall. An open window, painted in dark brown, is cut behind the figure. The bare body of the orange-and-red man has both arms hanging stiff at his sides, as if it might be dangerous to touch the walls or lean against the window. Two red, inverted pyramids, one pointing up and one down, adorn the man's body. These dark pyramids reminded me of the black lines on the white wall of the hacienda, the trapped figure crying for a way out—my imagination running with me as I stared at Tamayo's painting in the museum and saw a way into the locked room. As a young poet in the mid-1970s, fresh from my curiosity over the hacienda, I saw the way in. But the way to the wall where the cross once hung suddenly vanished from my mind as my friend distracted me by pulling me toward another painting. We got excited and threw lines of poetry at each other, trying to show off to see which one of us was better at reciting favorite poems by Robert Bly or James Wright or Galway Kinnell. I tried to memorize Pablo Neruda once and fell flat on my face. That day in the museum, my friend, who was better at this, led me away from the key to getting into the hacienda. Again, this was more than thirty years ago. Perhaps he didn't do it on purpose; we were thrilled at the Tamayo exhibit. Perhaps he did it because the early process of discovering poetry and visual art is one where many things are marked or carved into the walls of memory and the imagination, but very few stay there.

In his essay "Transfigurations," from a book on Mexican painters, the great poet Octavio Paz describes Tamayo's art as "a system of summonses and answers and humans are still part of the earth. They are the earth." Paz goes on to say that Tamayo's exaggerated style of painting human forms standing by windows and walls, with their grotesque bones, arms, and legs, leads to them representing "transmission channels, establishing communication between Tamayo and the world of his childhood." Walls and arches, windows and shelters, the human form wanting to get out and wanting to be kept in, as if the aromas of smelling salts and a wet towel on the forehead will release the fainted boy and let him fly past the confining spaces of home. The windows and doors are open under the arches, and Tamayo's disfigured humans are grasping for a way out, too. Paz concludes his discussion of Tamayo by insisting that "the artist is the person who has not entirely buried his or her childhood."

Each stone is the face of magic. Some stones get dislodged from their holes. Each storm lags, then explodes over houses, pounding the dry roofs with rain, soaking the adobe until its surfaces spring wet bruises, until the windows and doors are finally thrown open so those inside can open their eyes and breathe. What is common happiness but a way out the door? The heat was predicted, and so was the shame. Mothers love precious metals to hang on their sweating chests. They hang there until flowers wither and die. Each stone is a primitive brain at rest. The tribe thought it was funny and left them there. It is amazing to search among the cracks in the adobe for an alphabet. It is wonderful to think about chicken and beans on the table. What makes us leave the hacienda are trees that won't fall on their own. The house is afraid, and there is a shovel leaning in a closet inside the vast house, but I can't see it, yet how do I know it is there, its metal rusting over the decades? Each stone on the dirt ground in the courtyard is the face of someone who left me alone.

Every morning, barefoot children dive into the radioactive waters of the Rio Grande, their parents holding the international bridge hostage in protest over the right to live. When the bridge is opened again, some will die and some will cross without fear. Each time the sun comes up, streets in El Paso lead to the top of the mountain where a tall, concrete Christ dies on the cross. Pilgrims trek up there and sometimes disappear.

When the day is the day, the river changes course and moves through the valley of labor and rows of black trees. When chili is picked, the fields turn blood red, the man with his black dog still walking across them toward me. What is gathered is lost. What disappears is found under the arches of the oldest church in town. Headless men are seen in doorways, their headless women lighting fires in the ovens of the blackest rooms. Every afternoon, people arrive to inhabit old houses boarded up for years, their cars hot to the touch, the roads across the desert leading them here. Some will stay, some will keep going before it is too late to cross la frontera. None of them is me.

Each evening, pictographs on the rocks leave new messages by changing shape before fading with the wind. What the symbols mean is known only to those who were born here and have never left. Each night, bats fly out of the roof of the mighty white building to escape wherever they have been, their flight into the canyons weaving a darkness toward the new morning that brings a sky that passes beyond the border and takes history away like the cross was taken away, like the fact that the lines of ash marking where it hung are finally going to disappear.

My Tamayo poem has vanished. I can't find it in my dozens of notebooks, their yellowing pages refusing to yield the page or date or moment I wrote the poem. I even search in an old trunk that contains silly poems I wrote in high school before I knew what poetry was all about. I keep searching for the Tamayo poem I wrote in challenge to Gary and his better poem. I rarely lose old poems and am careful to the point of being fanatical about saving everything. I can't find the Tamayo poem because the arch of memory doesn't gravitate to the geometric spot where I can possibly recall it or rewrite it. Instead, I find a poem dated a few days after the initial 1978 visit to the abandoned hacienda:

> I have a finger on the thorn and I hold the blue lizard.
> I have its tail and its two eyes, the start of the journey
> and the cross on the hill that stands between
> the shoulders of the river that flows nowhere.
> I have a finger on the cross and I have a silence
> that sings and signs its name.
> I have a trail to an adobe wall that sinks into the earth
> to touch my grandmother that lies under the lying stones.
>
> I have a finger on her long, white hair
> that braids the earth.
> I have her looks and her speech, the taste of dust that
> blessed things that moved before movement within these walls
> was outlawed by the shining blue lizard that
> sprung out of my hands.

Someone walked under the arches and found the writings of the madman. In the text, you are standing under the trees. Hernán Cortés had sixteen horses, but they were killed by the frightened Aztecs. When the butterfly landed on your shoulder, you sat on the park bench and waited for another. *The Lone Ranger* is your earliest image of childhood TV, but there was also a blank screen and tumbling doors. A woman climbs the stairs in Emily

Dickinson's house, her husband downstairs two months from leaving her. On the other side of the bridge you crossed was a child with no legs, begging for coins. When Basho stood at the gates of the emperor, two frogs leaped out of his robe and entered first. Someone uncovered a photo of the saint. In reciting his prayer, you forgot three words, but found them scratched under the arch. The day you left town, the scarecrow was torn down from your uncle's field. When you thought joy was hidden in things you loved, someone called your name in a language you didn't know. The first person to comprehend Salvador Dali's final painting disappeared two days after seeing it. A man crossed the street after finding your name in the library, thought about his wife, and was hit by a car. On the other side of the house where you grew up, they uncovered an ancient burial site and built a highway. When you arrived at the last church you ever entered, everyone was kneeling, and no one looked up.

Paz insists on the memory of childhood, but he is talking about the waking state, the condition I would be in if I could step inside the hacienda to erase the black lines and allow the whole place to glow radiant and white. Standing under the arches, I smell the murals of Diego Rivera and the burning guitar of Jimi Hendrix, smell the fish Christ refused at the feast and the beer breath of my grandfather, dead for sixty-two years, the flowers at my grandmother's funeral, and the last meal my father ate before he abandoned my mother. I smell the smoke of an extinct volcano and the paint on the face of Moctezuma, the open hands on the outstretched arms of la Virgen de Guadalupe, and the jet fuel of our worst nightmares.

I smell the stinking feet of my father at the end of his working day and the electric wires behind my computer, the oily rag Miles Davis used to shine his trumpet, and the polish on John Coltrane's shoes. I can still smell the perfume of my first girlfriend in high school, the desert after a quiet rain, the mud on the drowned man pulled out of the Rio Grande, and the incense in Chairman Mao's private brothel. I smell the onion of Miguel Hernandez's starving son, the holy water of the last church I set foot in, the sweat of the son I never had, the clay on Alberto Giacometti's hands, the gunpowder on the border patrolman's pistol, and the plums William Carlos Williams wanted to eat.

I smell the dust on the yellow family photos from 1923 and the last bath I took before I grew up, the plaster on the death mask of Pancho Villa, the mosquito repellent I used when I finally climbed the canyon and wrinkled my nose at the clear air before a rattlesnake strike. I smell the ink on the typewriter where I wrote my first poems and the glue in my old scrapbook of rejection slips, the shampooed hair of the woman who loves me and the trash can where I threw away notes no one could read, the tortured feet of San Martín de Porres, the glowing ashes of a fallen saint.

I smell the shit of the parrot I had when I was four years old, the scent of the wet feather that fell on my sleeping head, the sulfur of the ghost I can never see, the dark room where my grandmother died, the empty canyon I couldn't climb and the seashells in Pablo Neruda's house, the engine of the car that took me away from El Paso for good. I smell the first snow I ever saw in my life and the summer grass of a house where I never belonged, the lightning that hit the tree half a block from my childhood home, fumes of a life I would live.

Back to the raised arm, the undergrowth of doubt and forced worship, shadows dancing tired and mistaken for justice in the pines. Back to the bitter twig, the thorn kiss, simple form of rain upon the bended knees of the ancestor who felt the strike against the holy wall before he let go of the twisted cross embedded between his shoulder blades.

I watch these walls wither and pray to the white world of plaster, adobe, and the crumbling maps that spread over the locked dwelling. I am locked out, and I am free to watch these walls wither as if the yucca also dies, to decide that nothing leaves except the cicada. As I walk slowly to my car, I yearn for the tamale hands of my grandmother, as if their actions of smearing these walls ever took place and I woke up one more time after passing out, opened my eyes after the final fainting spell of my young life, turned to the wall near the door to my grandmother's bedroom, and got my eyes to focus by staring at the crucifix on her wall.

Part Three

The Ladybugs

I walk into my university office the day after the World Trade Center attacks. Classes were canceled the previous afternoon, and I have not had a chance to talk to any of my students since the terror. I set down my book bag, turn to my desk, and notice a ladybug crawling up my shirt, its tiny red body moving over the buttons on my chest. My first impulse is to flick it off, but I like ladybugs and consider them signs of good luck. I gently place my fingertip in its path, and the insect climbs aboard. I sit down and watch it move across my finger, then onto the desktop. Distracted by having to get ready for class, I flip through my lecture notes and check my e-mail. When I turn back to the desk, the ladybug has disappeared. I search under papers and files, but it is gone. I don't want it harmed or crushed by a book, but where did it go?

I try to imagine how far I carried it on my clothes, when the exact moment of its landing on me took place. These thoughts in search of precise time come from the hours I spent in front of the television the previous day. After a while, the unforgettable images of the collapsing towers melted into exact moments of horror, the news commentators repeating what happened at what moment and at what human cost. My ladybug has vanished, its invisible ride on me a microscopic act in a world where it seems like each tiny thing we do has now been amplified by fire and fear.

I bring up the subject of the terrorist attacks in my undergraduate nature-writing class, but no one wants to join in. I manage to connect the optimism that nature writers present in their work with a sense of hope for the future in light of the terrorism. I insist that nature literature is the kind of writing we should read in a shocking time. Torn between discussing Henry Thoreau and talking about thousands of deaths, I look at the thirty students huddled in the small room. They stare at me in silence, events in the outer world pressing against the old, ugly walls of the building. Even the students who regularly contribute to discussions are quiet. As teachers, do we allow this sudden tragedy to come into our classes, or do we try and shut the door? It seems the attacks have entered during the first day of school after the tragedy, but we don't know how to proceed. How will a catastrophic event affect my lesson plans and the way young people, never having known an environment of war, respond to the assigned readings? It is too much to ponder as I stand in front of them and awkwardly get back to the sanctuary of Walden Pond.

Has the subject I'm teaching influenced their silence? Has Thoreau's pastoral idealism dictated a quiet atmosphere among these students? Perhaps history and political science classes are reacting in more vocal ways as I analyze Thoreau's reasons for wanting to touch a loon, for even becoming the bird in one of the better-known chapters of *Walden*. Transcendentalism and Thoreau's warnings to his fellow New England citizens not to abandon an essential harmony with nature appeal to the students. We wind up having a lively discussion about the loon in the pond and why Thoreau insisted that hunting without a gun was one way to move beyond the boundaries of civilization—a belief that fell on deaf ears. There is enough time left in the period to discuss another famous passage in *Walden*—the battle between the red and black ants Thoreau gathered in a jar. I exhaust every metaphor about armies, good and evil, and human behavior in a time of war. The session ends as we isolate transcendence with the loon and nature's violent character as two key lessons for our time. The students pile out of the room, and I feel a sense of triumph and relief. Several of them connected the previous day's events with the timeless lessons of environmental literature.

I stand alone in the empty classroom and can't forget the images on campus from the previous day. When classes were canceled on the eleventh and I walked across campus to my car, I saw dozens of students in tears. Many of them were huddled in small groups, cell phones in hand, a few hugging each other as they cried. The day after, I stroll the three blocks to the parking garage in silence, passing dozens of students and seeing that the fear and uncertainty are still on their faces. I reach my car on the fourth level of the massive garage after having momentarily forgotten where I parked that day. I unlock the door, throw my book bag on the seat, and climb in. As I reach for the magnetic card that will open the gate on the ground level, I spot a ladybug moving across my bag. Is it the same one that appeared in my office? My bag was on a chair near my office door, and I never set it near the desk where the first ladybug appeared. Can this be a second ladybug and another sign of good luck? Why would I be getting these kinds of clues in the midst of a terrible and frightening time? Where are the ladybugs coming from? I rarely see them at other times of the year. Instead of allowing the ladybug to disappear inside my car, I roll down the window, place my finger in the path of the insect on my bag, and watch as it climbs on. I shake my finger outside, and the ladybug flies away in a miniature dot of light.

I sit in my car for several minutes, not wanting to leave yet. The garage is located one block from the edge of campus, so the bustle and activity of thousands of students are muted. An eerie silence hangs among the rows of parked cars and concrete pillars. They remind me of the towers and how I finally had to turn off the television. The class discussion on Thoreau and his ideas on wilderness and the encroachment of civilization rings in my ears, yet they seem so far away. He was writing about America in the mid–nineteenth century and tried to encourage people to pause from their hard work on their farms and look around. The power of nature in its wild state on the continent had not yet been diminished by a great nation. One hundred and fifty years later it seems the only wildness we know is one of crushed concrete, elusive enemies, and a state where the survival of our way of life has nothing to do with the natural power of the earth.

I pull out of the garage and turn onto the street leading to the freeway I take to get home. As I emerge from the shelter of the ramp, sunlight flashes across the windows and lights up the car. At that moment, I spot a ladybug clinging to the windshield on the outside directly at my eye level. It stays on the glass as I turn into traffic. My impulse is to slow down, but I have increased my speed to keep up with the other cars. As I switch lanes, the ladybug springs off the windshield, its flared wings the purest fire I have imagined that day.

We Forget Who We Are

A wild rabbit eats blossoms from my wife's garden, appearing each night as everyone is asleep. It rains for days, and there is no news about the weather. The country buries a past leader, his funeral reminding some of us that the darkness and abuse of power never die. A legendary soul singer also passes away, his nine children and seven wives avoiding the spotlight. The appearance of the coyote at the top of the desert hill surprises me when it comes back to wake me, though the other recent dream I truly recall has me volunteering to wash dishes in a homeless shelter.

My students defend their isolation inside their iPod headphones, hundreds of them walking across campus, others too busy on their cell phones to plug themselves in. To think deeply terrifies some of them, but all I can do is recall the border town where I grew up, the blowing sands of memory covering details that refuse to come back. A young man I taught keeps an old copy of Woody Guthrie's writings, rechecking it out of the library again and again, waiting for the claim slip that says he has to give it up after two years of carrying it in his knapsack.

The death and destruction symbolized on the walls at Cochiti Pueblo fold into stone that can't be moved. A local old poet, a legend in his time, publishes a book of poems against the war in Iraq, but who will listen outside his circle of followers? Nothing changes as new mass-transit trains thread their way through the city, hundreds of curious passengers boarding for their first ride to the mall.

I consider filing a discrimination lawsuit against my university, but no one wants to hear the details. A teaching position at a major university, with its many perks, is a cozy job, though foreign species are destroying the ecosystem of the Great Lakes, fish such as the Eurasian ruffe, the Round goby, and the Silver carp overpopulating the region, their poisoned bodies eaten by birds and other wildlife, whose carcasses keep washing up on shore. I have not seen my father for several years, my parent's divorce of two decades ago creating two worlds. My mother, three sisters, and I dwell in the first, but the second world where my father, the stranger, lives goes unnamed, unknown, undescribed. There are dozens of pine cones lying in the grass under a huge tree. I can't forget that image, the grassy hill containing the lone pine, its seeds scattered about as a young man walks up the slope into the shade of its branches. A man stands right on the U.S.–Mexican border, and he is confused. He stands on the international bridge between two countries and looks out over the Rio Grande. He is confused because both cityscapes look the same from the bridge. He does not know where he is, but will not step deeper into Mexico. He turns toward the United States and does not want to go back. He hesitates on the border, making sure his feet are directly on the line. He is between countries and does not know where to step next.

I follow the lines of memory, but don't want to see them as memory any longer. They have become the images I keep focusing on, people rising and moving and coming toward me as if they have never left and have always known me. I wait in those thoughts as if I have never moved from that past moment that is the present and will always be the future. Some people claim they have heard the noise of the Creator and know what it means. The poor, brilliant boy lost in the dirt streets of Juárez hears the sound and moves closer to taking care of his hunger. The narrow alley winds between adobe walls painted turquoise, pink, and green. The barefoot boy hears the sound and stops before a dark doorway, a torn shawl hanging there as a curtain. He thinks he hears the distant sound of an electric fan and smells the aroma of fresh-baked tortillas. When he knocks on the door, dizzy in the heat, no one answers, so he enters into the coolness of the room. The empty kitchen waits in darkness as the boy stops before the wooden table and stares at the stack of tortillas steaming in an open clay bowl.

I used to see a man walking like an angel in the cottonwoods along the Rio Grande. I thought he could be my lost uncle Jose, missing forty-five years, or the priest from El Calvario Church who said boys like me were wrong—that there was nothing moving behind the rows of candles at the altar. Suddenly, among those dark branches extending over the river, I

heard a voice calling across the water, but I knew it was not looking for me.
When I moved closer, I startled a sleeping dove, the clattering of its wings
taking me to its hidden nest, where I saw what I had never seen—strings
of light giving birth to the tiniest things that sent me away, those heavy
limbs bristling in shadows that punished me by revealing where the man
stepped here and there. For the cottonwoods, I would believe this and go
there to hide as a boy. For those same dying trees forty years later, I would
go there and watch shadows replace the giants of childhood—groves of
enormous trunks that will rise in the desert sun even after the cottonwoods
are gone. So rarely now do I go to those trees with justice and the scent
of the deprived eye that searches for what I should see—a hungry bark
peeling off the branches, the knot in the trunk twisting into a fist that will
open for me. When I do go there, how can it be? The river is mad and
brown, speeding toward the southern horizon as if the age of mighty trees
is lost forever. Even the vultures and the lone sparrow hawk don't land on
the branches as I used to spot them as a child. When I go there, what is
the gift of an unexpected splinter in my palm after I rub the closest trunk,
then turn and walk away? So often in the cottonwoods I used to see a man
standing there like an angel forgotten in the wind. At times, he would point
to the sky bristling through the branches, and I could see. This time, it
could finally be him, but all that is rooted there now is the ancient rhythm
of those trees.

A legendary rock musician is ridiculed for doing commercials for women's
underwear. The current president is busy destroying his administration as
his cohorts try to destroy the world. A young poet writes a book about
his homeless father, whom he met only three times in thirty years. The
last time the writer saw his father was when he worked in a soup kitchen
and his father happened to be one of the street people being served. I read
this in a newspaper about one week after having that dream about volunteering in the kitchen of a similar shelter. Why are the poets dreaming of
and creating around the idea of homeless, rootless fathers? Is it old news?
Another writer, old and obscure, though well published, once wrote in a
now out-of-print book, "Lao-Tse, who was of supernatural conception, was
carried in his mother's body for sixty-two years. That is why his hair was
white at birth."

Steps continue into the cave where the population of Mexican free-tailed
bats is down from a peak of three million to less than three hundred thousand. They still fly out of the cave each evening, their beeping in the atmo-

sphere picked up by a radio antennae towering among the rocky cliffs in Socorro, New Mexico. Someone once told me you can predict the future by the way cottage cheese coagulates in those plastic tubs you buy in supermarkets. I laughed, but the man who told me this never saw me as his friend and disappeared. This must have been more than ten years ago. Birds emerged through a black window in the old mansion, a boarded-up house at the top of the hill in my neighborhood, the enormous gray structure the former home of a witch all the boys used to talk about, daring each other to go up to her house and throw rocks at the door. There was a rumor that she caught one of the boys once and poured jars of honey on the screaming youth, the sweet river covering his head and shoulders as she released hundreds of bees from special screened cages where their hives hung. We wanted to believe that the boy and his military family left school because his father was reassigned elsewhere, but the whispers about the witch and her honey persisted for a while in my elementary school, until the boy was forgotten. I don't know what happened to the witch or how long she lived. I never saw her.

There is a black caterpillar on the porch, its black hairs weaving the air so I can admit there is growth in what I have done. No one told me it would take this long for the old friend to arrive. He has kissed his mother good-bye too often. Black caterpillar eating the herbs in the garden, swallowing the scent of what went wrong. No one judged me when I guarded my home from the intricate approaches—the loam, the mulch, the ways we cradle what grows as if we are the makers who can speak to the plants. I once lifted a different caterpillar on my shovel, its heavy tube of hair flying through the air as I tossed it away, thinking it would never return. An angry bumblebee flew at me in return, its thick yellow-and-black ball hitting the roof of the house and buzzing away. I thought about crushing this second caterpillar, but had no way of knowing what would squeeze out of its body, if it would smear my hands with what I couldn't admit.

I water the earth constantly with my garden hose to watch and learn. Dung beetles, black widows, strawberries eaten out by ants, tiny tomatoes taking forever—how can the black wasp disappear into the wall when every flying insect has been accepted as coming and going without cost? Why was the bumblebee so loud and fast? Did it escape the witch? My feet suddenly sink in the mulch. A tiny yellow spider sprints under a leaf. Where is the tomato plant I replanted here weeks ago? I look down as the white worm encircles itself in the soil, sticking to my shovel like the glue one root created in its manner of curing because this worm has nothing to do with the hairy, black caterpillar tracing its life across the porch.

I come back to find the students are gone and the books forgotten. The empty hallways of academia ferment resentment, jealousy, and a racist atmosphere I wrestle with constantly. This sounds ridiculous, perhaps an old civil rights cry from the 1960s, a period I teach often in my "Literature of Rock and Roll" class, but it is merely a description of the mighty university where I work. What does this have to do with the Nahua poet who stands at the top of the mountain and screams his poem at the clouds? There is no one else up there with him. He is alone and rapidly ascending into the waiting clouds. When the listening clouds pass over him, it rains and rains, and this surprising fall of water is not what he had been praying for. He wanted the sunlight instead.

They say the temple still stands, but my friend on the West Coast is paralyzed in bed, the medication affecting him deeply, his unexpected struggle making him ponder the end of his days. This is nothing new for any of us, but as he gets better and is able to sit and walk around his quiet home, the thoughts he had about how many planets remain undiscovered in the universe keep bothering him. Is it the medication? He drinks a glass of milk in his kitchen, the sweat pouring down his bare chest. When the phone rings, it is a wrong number, and he wonders who the hell "Nicky" is because the caller asked, "Is Nicky there? Is this Nicky?"

The feral hog population in East Texas is out of control, wildlife scientists warn, and one rancher said he was afraid to let his grandchildren leave the yard. A Minnesota newspaper reports that the wild boar population along the Mississippi and Minnesota rivers is growing and that more of the enraged beasts are attacking people and their pets. It is the Age of the Pig, but I have not yet seen any media pieces on that idea.

Astrophysicists suggest that a highway of dark matter ripped from the dwarf galaxy Sagittarius, which is being consumed by the Milky Way, is streaming right through Earth. Sagittarius? It reminds me of my recent focus on the 1960s and its music. Remember the Age of Aquarius? How about the ripped Sagittarius as the dying movement on the left, millions refusing to march in the streets against the war in Iraq? Let's say the Milky Way is the fundamentalist, right-wing force that controls this country. The heavens are falling apart, victims of eternal divisions. But what is that highway of dark matter cutting right through us? Does it contain Bibles, flags, pledges of allegiance, Enron-rich boys, and military guides expert in the art of torture? Where will the dark matter go when the "evil empires" on the other side of the earth have supposedly crumbled? It is a highway cutting through the core of the mountain, casting old deserts, canyons, and weak adobe dwellings into the dust of naive and idealistic childhood dreams. When it comes out on the other side, bounces off the galaxy, and turns right around in its ricochet toward us, it is time to leave home because personal history and any view about justice struggle for air in the vacuum of outer space.

The Ku Klux Klan members on the evening news wave their flags and scream under the hoods. Someone will remember this when hatred under the Texas sky becomes a great rain of blood. Someone will know the identity of every man, woman, and child under the white sheets. They remind me of the guys in high school who surrounded me, called me "dumb Mexican," made me walk the line between them as they hit me. I thrived on it out of fear. It was my identity in the crowded halls of the school, my dance at the pep rally, my way of avoiding the spotlight when they arrested two of them for breaking into the school. The KKK members in the state capitol understand America. They know that white sheets cover the blood of generations, give them reason to come burning in the night like an old movie where the lynching was real. Walking home from high school, I once saw two boys fighting, the Chicano beating the crap out of the white guy who used to be the local bully. Days later I heard four guys got Carlos with bats and two-by-fours. It was the first time I was glad it wasn't me, the quiet, fat one who never fought back but knew how to survive like the silence of the TV screen where the white sheets come back, the hate I saw back then the same hate I see now—white sheets, swastikas, and burning crosses the same colorful graffiti that rained blood in the hallways and classrooms of school.

When Bob Dylan unstrapped his acoustic guitar after recording a few songs for *Blood on the Tracks*, he forgot the other two songs he had been carrying in his head. When he picked up the guitar in the studio again, he wrote a different song that never made it on the record, though the two forgotten songs appear on bootlegs. The last guitar John Lennon played before he was murdered stood against the cold fireplace in his New York apartment, the leather collar he wore on the cover of *Two Virgins* tied around its neck. When Eric Clapton's four-year-old son fell out of a forty-ninth-floor apartment to his death, there were two electric and two acoustic guitars in the room with the open window.

The guitar Pete Townshend smashed at Monterey in 1967 was salvaged for parts in a London shop, the instrument shipped back in pieces from California. The guitar Jimi Hendrix burned at Monterey was never seen again after the show, his roadies claiming for years that it simply vanished backstage. When Patti Smith performed her last concert before her husband Fred suddenly died, the guitar she played that night was a pure white Stratocaster. After the last gig Mick Abrahams played with Jethro Tull, he sold four of his guitars and did not play for two years. The last time Jimmy Page used a violin bow on his Les Paul, the friction between the bow and the guitar strings disintegrated the bow halfway through the song.

Two days before blowing himself away, Kurt Cobain threw seven electric guitars into the street outside his Seattle home, keeping five acoustic guitars in the bedroom where he slept for the last time. In his coat closet, Lou Reed found a guitar he had not seen in years, the red instrument leaning against the back of the closet, a black T-shirt draped over it. Joni Mitchell lost two dark purple guitar picks on stage the last time she played a song from *Blue*, signaling a roadie for another after the two picks flew from her strumming fingers into the audience. Before taking the outdoor stage in Mexico City, in front of a crowd of eighty thousand, Carlos Santana knelt before three unplugged electric guitars, rubbed herbal oil up and down the frets, wiped the moisture with a cloth, then stuck three rosary beads on the guitars, one bead per instrument embedded in a tiny hole he had had someone drill in each solid body. When the first print for the cover of George Harrison's *All Things Must Pass* was developed, it showed a guitar lying in the grass near the elves surrounding George. He swore there was no guitar, and the photo was reshot, the second showing the elves without the guitar. A biographer of the Beatles later claimed Harrison told him the first photo contained one of the first guitars he played in the group, an instrument he had sold years before leaving the band and recording his first solo album. The guitar photo is somewhere in the Harrison archives.

Joe Strummer used the same acoustic guitar on his three Mescalero albums, his last work before dying. The last time Neil Young played "Like a Hurricane" in concert, his rare black Les Paul produced feedback that burned a dark line across the forehead of a fan who was leaning on the stage in front of Neil. She never knew where it came from and couldn't wash it off. Her doctor told her it could lead to skin cancer and that she needed to stay away from tanning beds. An unknown Tommy Bolin was sixteen years old when he jumped onstage barefoot at a Grateful Dead concert in Denver, jamming with the band on several songs. Two days later, someone broke into his Boulder apartment and stole his only guitar, the young musician at that time having less than ten years to live.

Peter Green had a nervous breakdown halfway into Fleetwood Mac's 1968 tour of the United States. The day it happened, he awoke in a New York hotel to find that each of his three guitars had one broken string. He spent the day restringing them and screaming at roadies, until everyone left him alone in his room. When he didn't show up for the sound check, the crew found an empty room and several guitar strings bristling on the floor. Jerry Garcia dreamed about his cut-off finger only twice in his life. The first time was on his thirty-fifth birthday, which was the day he took four acid tabs. The second dream came years later, the night after the Dead played a forty-five-minute version of "Dark Star" and Jerry switched guitars half an hour into the song. The second dream was of a white guitar with silhouettes of his finger tattooed all over the shiny instrument.

One day after quitting the Yardbirds, Jeff Beck plugged his Les Paul into brand-new Marshall amps and blew them out without playing a note. When he pulled the plug, a blue spark shot up his right hand. Frank Zappa fired off a fiery solo in the middle of "Black Napkins," his bare chest covered in sweat, his tight bell-bottom trousers now soaked, his feet moving across the stage in huge platform shoes, the crowd teasing Frank, a girl throwing paper flowers, Frank grabbing a pink rose in midair and stuffing it between the many dials and buttons on his guitar, the ridiculous act of a fan throwing paper flowers making Frank turn his back to the audience to let out a tremendous fart no one heard under the heavy wall of sound his band was laying down. Duane Allman saw the truck cross his path the instant before his motorcycle slammed into it, the bright flash forming his last thought, which was the realization that he had two dark purple guitar picks in his jacket pocket.

Emmylou Harris strummed her guitar in the overpowering lights of the tiny club, her first public performance of "Boulder to Birmingham," a song about Gram Parsons, taking place before an audience of sixty people, fourteen of them guitar players. Five years earlier Keith Richards lent a strung-out Gram a guitar so he could sit in on the *Exile on Main Street* sessions. Gram's contributions to several songs were erased by the Stones, though Keith stole a great guitar solo from Gram and used it on a later song. The last time Gram played live on stage, he noticed how many people were lighting cigarettes in the dark club, the tiny flames of their lighters flickering across the room and reflecting on the smooth body of his brand new guitar.

I thought I had experienced the last one, but the first rattlesnake dream in months took me to a wide field of dirt, a flat terrain of dust and wind. A small house stood atop a pile of boulders and several flat, oval rocks that rose like natural steps toward the house. Suddenly, I was inside with Manny Cordova, an old friend from high school I had not seen in thirty-six years. He was a wrinkled old man with long, white hair, his torn and simple eyes staring at me. He went out onto the rocky ledge that surrounded the house and pointed to the ground without a word. I saw two gigantic rocks below, with hundreds of snakes swarming over them—coiling snakes of many colors slithering in and out of the rocks. Manny climbed down and went to the rock on the left. It was filled with huge turtles the size of dogs, huge desert crawlers that loved Manny. He lay down in the middle of the enormous turtles, rubbed their bellies, and ran his hands over their ancient shells. He laughed and played with them as if they were pets that loved to be rubbed down, hundreds of rattlers coiling around him, but not striking at him or the turtles. I found myself at the bottom of the rocks, the house above me. Manny became one of the turtles and disappeared into the mass. Manny appeared as a human again, rising from his bed of turtles to ask me if I were going to climb up the rocks and go into the house. It was the first time he had spoken. Snakes moved everywhere as I tried to climb up. I grabbed onto a flat red stone. It was loose, and I lost my grip. In the dream, I was suddenly in my bed and threw the blankets aside to find a snake under them. It was not a rattler, but looked like a coral snake. I started to panic and cried out, then woke myself with a familiar sound of yearning.

He doesn't believe in miracles, tells me that fathers never return and that mothers write secret books throughout their lives. One hundred and four degrees in El Paso, and the house of childhood solitude is still there. "Have you heard the one about the two-headed lizard?" he asks. I nod without a word and wonder why I have returned. "Do you know the story about the pages in the yellow, tattered book that wouldn't open?" he keeps asking. "The old glue kept them stuck together, and the secret you were looking for was right in there." I turn to him and want to ask him how he knows all this weird stuff, but don't feel like probing into the dusty shelves in my mother's house, most of the books from my youth and high school years thrown out decades ago. Then he gets serious, sits me down by the fireplace in the living room my mother hasn't used in about thirty years, and whispers, "I suggest you avoid the Deeves, which wander across the Chihuahua Desert uttering horrible cries. You will recognize them by their horns and tails, resembling those of animals. Avoid them, but if you do run into one, remember they have powerful magic." Before I can laugh and tell him to shut up, he vanishes and leaves me alone in my mother's house.

A picture guide to key buildings of the twentieth century leaves out my grandmother's house in El Paso, where I was born. It is the lone standing house under the concrete pillars of a freeway that destroyed several blocks of the old neighborhood. Ovid's *Metamorphosis* in a new translation leaves out my lack of desire to read it and attempt to understand it. *The Great Secrets: True Stories about Famous Historical Mysteries* is about disputed identities and wonders if the son of Louis XVI and Marie Antoinette really died in the Temple Tower and asks who Kaspar Hauser was. Was he an abused child, the crown prince of Baden, or a pathological liar? Flipping through it, I look for the case of Emilio Canales, the Mexican revolutionary hero who fathered thirty-two children by thirty-two women. Yes, that is correct. After each woman gave birth to the first child by Emilio, he would not sleep with her again and kept careful records of the pregnancies. What about Lorenza Chavez, who gave birth to two desert turtles in 1923, each dark green thing coming out of her as she screamed in the tiny barrio clinic of South El Paso? When the doctor dropped the turtles in a bloody pan, their hard shells made a loud noise. "Where is the father?" the doctor demanded. Twenty-four-year-old Lorenza looked up through tears of pain and shock and said, "He left me three months ago after he found a two-headed lizard in our bedroom and killed it. He threw it into the trash can in the alley behind our house, and I never saw him again."

A mole can dig a tunnel three hundred feet long in a single night. As I think about this, I spot an odd-looking insect clinging to the back-door screen. I have never seen such a creature, and its appearance in this early, cool spring tells me something is up because the last time I saw an insect I couldn't identify, I went blind for a few days. I step closer to the door to have a good look, which makes the dark-colored thing buzz for an instant, then settle back onto the screen. I squint and study it. I can't tell if it is a beetle, some mad wasp, or a lost bug from some ancient past. Then I recall a crazy student of mine telling me that a turtle can breathe through its butt. I wrote all over his poems and gave him a bad grade, but it doesn't keep this insect from landing on my screen door weeks later.

I want to flick the screen with my fingers to get the bug to go away, but another quick buzz freezes me to the spot as the thing unfolds huge, diamond-shaped wings and stretches them against the wire screen as if showing off. I have never seen anything like it. Its form makes me think about the fact that owls have three eyelids. The first eyelid protects the eye, the second filters light, and the third shuts when the owl chooses you as its next victim, swooping down in the exact way this insect suddenly lifts into the air and starts bouncing against the screen. Tiny, wired pops resound through the early morning as this insane bug keeps bouncing against the screen, probably wanting to come in and do me harm. I pull back and notice a book on mammals on my bookshelf. It is a huge hardcover I opened once to find that sloths move so slowly that green algae grows in the grooves of their hair.

Algae in hair? All I have heard about is lice in crotch hair, as in the sloth who caught some from a stranger and told me about it—not in class like the student and his turtle lore, but some loser sitting next to me at a poetry reading. Maybe this bouncing insect that wants to tear a hole in the screen is an overgrown version of lice and other things people share with me. Secrecy has come home to roost in the form of this awful thing. It is one reason I stay home and try to live calmly in my basement library. This insect has changed that today. It alights on the screen again, huge wings folded, its dark blue body resembling a large, shiny marble. A dragonfly flaps its wings twenty to forty times a second, bees and houseflies two hundred times, some mosquitoes six hundred times, and a tiny gnat one thousand times. I learned these facts after the kid next door, a notorious brat, brought me a cicada whose legs he had enjoyed pulling off, one at a time. When I told him to go home, he threw the poor thing against my door. I stare at this motionless insect that won't leave. A housefly can transport germs as far as fifteen miles away from the original source of contamination, but I don't have time to worry about that because as I stare at the bug, I am shocked to see a fly actually appear near the screen, but this quieter pest is inside the house. I can't believe it. It is too early in the year for flies and bugs. As I go to the laundry room and grab a flyswatter my wife uses to swat our misbehaving male cat, I am glad I haven't seen any mosquitoes yet because a mosquito has forty-seven teeth. I smash the fly against the screen on my first try. What luck because this whack awakens the big insect, which lets off an incredible buzzing roar as it rises like a lost helicopter an invading army left behind. It disappears in the morning sun. I find the dead fly on the floor, shovel it up with the flyswatter, open the door, and hear a distant buzzing as I shake the swatter over the grass. By the way, a nest in which insects or spiders deposit their eggs is called a "nidus," but I have already shut the door.

Why do we pause when the days burn in yellow and green? Has it been fifteen years since we drove past the giant cliff at Shiprock, New Mexico? One hundred miles later, thousands of saguaros rose from the red rocks and surrounded us. When we gazed over the edge of the Grand Canyon, something moved across the river miles below. When the men in uniform stormed the cabin near the Mexican border, they broke down the door and found dozens of rusted rolls of barbed wire—nothing but neatly stacked, though rusted, rows of barbed wire. The oldest house in the United States is located in Santa Fe, New Mexico. It stands with the oldest church, held up since 1630 by the need to preserve what was destroyed. The oldest house is a museum, adobe ceiling sagging into the room where an Indian mummy sits in a chair, hand outstretched to hold the coins tourists drop. Its skull grins like a survivor presiding over the coffin across the room. Another Indian lies exposed, the coffin cut open to show the face of Alfonso Ruiz Quintana. He once lighted the fire in the oven to warm the believers who entered, protecting him from evil spirits hiding by the river. The face in the coffin belongs to the man who disobeyed the priests. We step into the room, can't ignore the skeletons propped to welcome us to a land where the revolt drove the conquistador away, giving it back to the silent ones who were dug up to prove the invaders were the last to leave. They built the church on the heaving chest of the woman giving birth to her son. He holds out his hand full of the coins that brought him luck and removed his master's eyes, ended the howling in the hills, and burned the trees where the birds gathered. He holds his hands out. The coins rattle a story where he was hung for being a liar, tortured and crucified by the priests for praying to birds with black wings. He was buried along the river to warn others that the muffled cries in this room belong to those who believe too much in the earth. We stand still and don't know where to look. Later, my wife will say her recent illness was caught in this corridor of cold sleep, spreading an unknown curse that forced us to go home coughing, wondering what source of shadow held the face that woke us hundreds of miles from home.

A wild rabbit eats blossoms from my wife's garden, appearing each night as everyone is asleep. It rains for days, and there is no news about the weather. Then, this morning, we stand in the kitchen window as two bright yellow birds peck at the white petals of the flowers, male and female chirping and dancing, even swimming in the bird bath as if the random bursts of color and vegetation are signals that the painter has returned. The two tiny birds spend a long time among the plants, my wife and I enjoying this display to forget the threat of the rabbit that is probably as hungry as the birds who alight in the grass and start pulling red worms out of the sod.

Under the leaves, the kiss of the snail. Hidden in the bricks, the whisper of spider webs spelling what went away. All things pray in the silence madness brings. You are recognized in the bringing when your father returns in a dream, his shoulder blades shields repelling love. He worked too hard, sweated in rivulets that left marks on a man, his ladder to the sky a sculpture from his labor. You have not said anything about the puzzle of two rivers, one tree, and twenty sad people who knew him. Under their photos, the touch of skin. Their tree does not falter, its shadows resembling what has not taken place. Somebody suddenly shouts, "The world ended yesterday. What are you doing here?"

They hope your answer arrives on time. How often do you count your toes before going to sleep? The great rooms are beautiful. You will remember them when it is time for a new house—walls of embers flying to tell us what you missed because the stars are tired of being written about. Many things are true when it is difficult to love the other, so stand on the earthly side. Walk against the road and listen to the crows call you, chords vibrating inside conch shells of living blood. Remove your hat because prophetic dreams are going to show pity on the boulevards, until they become streets of tenderness, memories of what followed you like stubborn scars on your arms.

The longest word used by Shakespeare in any of his works is *honorificabilitudinitatibus*. Believe me when I say it doesn't mean the lone black hair that sticks out of your big right toe just below the toenail. The word for that hair is *slypadorelystybold*. Pregnant goldfish are called "twits," but my father used to call me a dummy, a goofball, like those stinking mothballs in closets that held his four pair of golf shoes whose spikes dug into the closet carpet, a detail only I can remember because my *slarapin* is alive. In other words, my second heart—the one that resides inside my soul and beats for the past and is able to put these things together. *Graffito* is the little-used singular of the much-used plural word *graffiti*, but *manes* is not the plural for more than one moon because to mistake mane for moon would mean I could not rise in the middle of the night, suffering from insomnia, and be able to go write something about a moon I have not seen in months, my words glowing on my computer screen brighter than the graffito I thought I dreamed about when I heard that a friend of one of my nephews had been gunned down in a drive-by. *Narcissism* is the psychiatric term for self-love as in the lone artist compelled to ignore his masterpiece leaning on the canvas because the cracked mirror in his tiny apartment is showing him too many stark visions he has not been able to conjure up through the powerful fumes rising out of the dozens of tubes of oil paints that are squashed all over the floor. A language becomes extinct in this world every two weeks. A silence fills the halls every three months, its source a secret, its ability to envelop and slow down the development of rapture a completely natural and potent thing that is best avoided from dusk to dawn, though one vital moment appears on the border of light and darkness as if something is about to touch those of us who have even the slightest clue as to what is going on. In 1961, Italian artist Piero Manzoni packed his feces in cans, signed and mounted them, and then sold them as art. This story about the natural elements of man is a very common one, an epic no artist or writer is able to comprehend because the canned stuff is the purest form of artistic expression, the fact that it is imprisoned in a container an excellent metaphor about creative souls who will create anything in order to get from here to there without having to step on too much shit, without having to face the crap in their lives or acknowledge what their mighty and private visions are truly made of. Old story, open the can. In 1983, a Japanese artist, Tadahiko Ogawa, made a copy of the *Mona Lisa* completely out of ordinary toast. Well, there was a football player for the New York Giants with the nickname "Toast" because he was burned all the time for touchdowns. So what? Toast. Crossing one's fingers is a way of secretly making the sign of the cross. The gesture was started by early Christians to ask for divine assistance without attracting the attention of pagans. Crossing the toes is a way of secretly making sure you are still alive, the rare ability to cross your toes saying more than I can possibly say. When a baby octopus is born, it is about the size of a flea. I once saw a flea the size of an octopus, but it was dead. A slug has four noses. My memories have only one nose. Sixty-two degrees Fahrenheit is the minimum temperature required for a grasshopper to be able to hop. I have a brass statue of a grasshopper in my office, but it doesn't do me any good because the wise man called me once and said, "Grasshopper," and the awful world showed up instead. Fine-grained volcanic ash can be found as an ingredient in some toothpaste. So can blood. Some asteroids have other asteroids orbiting them. Some hemorrhoids have other hemorrhoids orbiting around them. Devoid of its cells and proteins, human blood has the same general makeup as sea water. I prefer the river.

Get on the Poetry Bus

I get on the poetry bus parked outside the downtown community college because my poem is on the bus and it is thirty years old. The long vehicle is painted a bright sky blue, and the two employees from Metro Transit stand on the open platform, looking bored. One of them is a black driver, and he probably wishes he were out on his normal run, instead of idling the bus on the street, waiting for the pack of poets to hop on board to "ooh" and "ahh" over the new posters containing their sacred words. I am one of those poets and am excited over a poetry event for the first time in years. As an old literary organizer, I've seen everything in the literary world and can't get too worked up anymore over public poetry events, but this is something else.

I want to express my enthusiasm with the young blonde who blocks the door of the bus, acting like the bored liaison between the bus company and the college that sponsored the local Poetry in Motion competition to select six poems for the city buses. She is busy staring at a couple of black kids who are being harassed by a Minneapolis cop at the end of the block. Next to them, a third black man who seems older than the two youths is standing in front of a card table he unfolded in the middle of the sidewalk and has spread his arms wide and high in the air. The cold wind of mid-April pushes a stack of his Jesus pamphlets off the table and onto the concrete.

"Did those kids try to rob him?" The blonde asks the driver as they both lean on the safety bars on either side of the door. They continue to block my path and stare at the scene on the curb.

They finally get out of my way, and I board as the cop says something to the two kids and points to the Jesus man, who is scrambling to pick up his pamphlets off the sidewalk. I don't care about them because I want to see my poem. I move down the aisle of the empty bus and look up at the colorful row of beautiful posters that will ride the city buses and transit train for the next two months in Minneapolis. I find my poem and stare at it, the incredible visual design that the graphics firm came up with for my poem knocking me out each time I gaze at it. I have to admit my poster is the best of the lot, and several people in the small audience we had for the earlier unveiling agree. I reach into my sweater pocket and finger the stack of bookmarks the coordinator of Poetry in Motion gave everyone. Until the actual posters arrive in the mail, I have to settle for the duplicates on the tiny bookmarks. I am impressed with the program, with the way all the poems were illustrated, and am happy to have one of my poems chosen.

The poets dance to a full moon because they don't know what else to do with themselves. They are tired of fighting and competing, weary from writing and seeing things no one else can see. The poets dance to a full moon because they know it will never last, their words of wisdom and insight temporary and fragile, their books unread and filed away by a vicious reading public that doesn't even know they exist. The poets dance to a full moon when it comes close to the earth, their visions of invincibility followed by those of madness—meandering moonlight illuminating their ways of survival and taking their breath away at the end of each poem, at a public recital, or at the peak of their powers. The poets dance to a full moon, and the arrogant ball grows bigger, deeper than their most common phrases, like "I love you, by the river, under the mountain, beyond the light." The poets dance to a full moon because its image controls their work—telling them when to rise and fall, when to love and hate, how to find the demon in the trees, and how to pretend they have touched God. When one or two start to get tired, their cloaks drenched in sweat, the dance takes a turn, a detour, the highway signs toward the full thing in the sky knocked over when the poets can't find inspiration, the moment they dread when the cycle is a moonless sky that doesn't take names. The poets dance to a full moon when the world threatens to end and their families stop talking to them, old lovers they never cared about appearing at the door one day, contract in hand. Strangers and familiar faces thrust limited copies before their faces, asking for a signature, a sign—appraising one or two favorite poems the poet hates, the rare edition going up in price upon the appearance of the X on the page. The poets dance to a full moon when the only notion to strike is the will to write, the calling from a dark chamber that doesn't know the moon, the placement of one foot before the other in the study where drawers of notebooks turn yellow for tomorrow's archives, the future's hidden domain no one will break open before the earthquake takes the library away. The poets dance to a full moon when childhood returns, and they must lecture the pain and the twisted moments away—fathers with leather belts, bullies with bloody knuckles, cold bedrooms in darkened houses with no one else around, the punishment for being who they are extending beyond midnight when no one comes home, unlocks the door, or puts them to bed. The poets dance to a full moon because it is time to grieve, time to say and repeat, this hour of kissing and hugging, moments of temporary despair turning to bright flowers screaming across the heavens to pollinate the moon with tomorrow's reams of paper. The poets dance to a full moon because no one knows them and they don't know themselves after the publication of their first books. They dance and dance and continue to write, one or two loving each other, three or four hating the power around them, wondering what took them there and how often it struck, why it was so deep and shattering, the lasting light coming from a thriving world with no moon.

I stare at the poster on the bus ceiling and imagine myself riding the bus to the university where I teach, looking up in the midst of a packed morning ride and joining other commuters in staring and reading what I wrote when I was twenty-three years old. Yes, that is correct. My poem "The Spirals of Dawn" was written in 1975 when I was finishing my undergraduate degree at UTEP. The poem became a part of my first manuscript, which wandered from small press to small press until it was published in 1985. The book went out of print in 1995, and as I stare at a poem I wrote more than half a lifetime ago, I wonder how the Poetry in Motion people found it. The short poem works for a poster and even has a line that became the title of one of my later books. I smile to myself and am actually self-conscious at liking this poster thing and the short reading I participated in earlier, where several of the winning poems were read and I told people I was emerging from my sabbatical to celebrate the unveiling with them. I get off the poetry bus as the driver and the blonde continue to wonder what the cop is doing with the two kids and why the third black man is letting the wind carry away so many of his pamphlets. His card table is almost empty, and there is no one, besides the kids and the cop trio, to take possession of the man's printed faith. Maybe if he put them on posters, they might last a great deal longer.

The following evening my wife and I go hear a legendary poet read in St. Paul. After years of doing rare public events, Gary Snyder emerges and is interviewed in a ridiculous radio format on the stage of a claustrophobic, ancient theater—the same site where a famous Minnesota icon does his weekly radio show that has become a national institution as it spits out the parts of Minnesota culture that make me want to hurl! I say this because as I watch a famous poet come out of hiding and go through the excruciating question-and-answer session at the hands of a radio host who knows nothing about poetry, I am reminded about the hypocrisy of a midwestern culture that tries to present itself as hip, aware, and in touch with the latest artistic trends, yet fumbles the ball constantly when it comes to presenting the traditions of various art forms.

We sit among five hundred people and get to stare at the woman host, who has worn a miniskirt and is showing her bare legs and thighs to the audience as she hits Snyder with superficial question after question. I didn't come out to watch this art babe turn a rare chance at hearing one of my favorite poets into another Minnesota version of cool. Snyder is professional, reads several poems from his latest book, and is patient with the embarrassing format. I paid lots of money for this? I get on the poetry bus by reminding myself that I had contacted Snyder several times in recent years in my attempts to bring him to the university where I teach. He turned me down three times, each response accompanied by the same short note—"No travel. No readings. No interviews. Gary Snyder." He and his wife had serious health problems in recent years, but he finally emerged, and I am here among an elderly crowd—old Snyder followers from the 1960s and 1970s, subscribers to the Talking Volumes series that brought him to town, and a few of the usual suspects from the Twin Cities poetry scene.

I hop off the bus when a local poetry publisher, notorious for being obnoxious and abusing his employees, spots me in the crowd and saunters up to me. "Ray, what are you doing here?" he asks, bewildered. I melt in my chair as he says, "I heard you were leaving town for good. What happened?"

"No," I answer as my wife glares at him. "I'm on sabbatical."

He nods in approval and wanders off without further word. I am quietly furious and make a mental note to myself to find out which poet, colleague, former student, or friend opened his or her mouth about my business—the topic is sensitive because of how close I came to filing a discrimination lawsuit against my university the previous year. I can't go into details because after the Snyder event, the poetry tide and the bus ride (those rhyme) lead me home to the seclusion of the suburbs.

The poet gazes at nothing and the poem arrives. Its hold is mighty and variable, designed to scatter his mind toward corners of experience he has not dusted in decades, though his heart carries them, year in and year out, slowing him down over time. He stops as he thinks about this approaching wave, a bothersome yearning that is finally here. Wait a minute, he thinks. How can the need to write about this slow me down when I need it so I can be a poet? The poem troubles his mind and senses as it hits him in the chest and rises into his psyche—that space poets cry over, reach for, and need to kiss like someone they will never see again. This poet is accomplished and knows how to take care of this wanted intrusion—to dedicate the language to what he sees and what he has done, twist it into a composition about something he never should have tried long ago, though he obviously survived.

The poet swims beyond the frontiers of occurrence and demolition—having destroyed the true encounter found long ago within the arriving poem. Its truths cannot serve him in their vital state because those conditions do not serve poetry. They merely mask the pure skin of poetic movement, blow the seeds of rapture away, and keep a distance between the poet and his sins. So he allows truth from an incident of twenty years ago to fade away, though the foundations for writing about it have hooked their claws into his neck for too long. As the time finally arrives, he has no choice but to reconstruct what once was, though he accepts the fact that he cannot duplicate the experience accurately. He lies and pulls fictitious moments out of his imagination, weaving the piece into a long poem that becomes one of his best in months. It is a relief because he has not had to wrestle with the language as long as he expected to. The poem is on the screen, its electric characters brimming with anger and cybermobilization—that despicable state he resents because it often stays ahead of his thoughts, sucking the words right out of his fingertips as he races across the keyboard. Whatever happened to notebook composition and the hand record of life?

As he sits there, he recalls that others have said there are no lies in poetry because those dimensions call for a different kind of truth—the specimen of existence found in the deepest bowels of the starving poet who must set the words down and get them to quit bouncing around in his head. So he adds a few more lines to his poem and feels better because he is not lying. He is in the field of poetic knowing, poetic skipping, a vast underground construction that moves his spine and skull to blast the poem onto the screen and commands him to print it out. There is no other way, and this is done without music, fanfare, or the desire to become better known. But what does fame have to do with this new poem that has finally shaken itself from his system? The poem is right there, beyond thought and desire as it shines on the neatly printed page. It might need work, some revision to clear away the cobwebs of time, but the poet sees it for the first time, and he feels lighter, at ease, despite its harsh subject.

"You can call my name." The poet looks up in his quiet study. The words sound again—"You can call my name." He glances quickly about, clutching the new poem in his right hand, forgetting to set it neatly on the stack of forty-eight other poems he has written in the past three weeks. Someone spoke. Someone called out to him. Someone is giving him a chance to reply, but he is immersed in the glory of his work, in the star of the white sheet—that muted applause that lifts speech away from his body and lets him live again. There is no one else in the room, so he goes back to his work because in a few hours he will have set enough distance between himself and this poem that its mighty forces will have stopped punishing him, will be unable to reach him because poem number fifty-two is coming together too easily.

The poet is trying to read his poems in a Borders Books in Albuquerque, one of the largest stores he has ever visited. The audience for his reading is one quiet high school girl and a man and woman who are talking loudly above the weak microphone the poet has been given. The man is standing with his back to the poet, who is at the edge of the café area where they stuck him. He has to read above the grinding espresso machine, the cash register, and the hum of people at the magazine racks ten feet behind him—the most popular spot in the store.

The man continues to talk to his woman friend, who is seated at a table in front of the poet. The man doesn't notice the poet is trying to start the reading by announcing over the mic, "Hello and thank you for coming." The high school girl pays attention, sees what the poet is going through, and winces for him. The bookstore is busy, and she is the only person there to hear him.

The poet glares at the back of the man who is talking louder to his woman friend. "Excuse me," the poet mutters weakly over the mic. The man does not turn around or stop talking. The poet is getting angry and turns to look for the staff person in charge of the readings. He is nowhere in sight, so the poet begins the reading by describing over the mic what his new book is about. As he does this, he erases half the poems on the list he prepared to read from. He fights the urge to tear the mic off its stand, put it close to his mouth, and shout to the man, "Hey, asshole! I'm trying to read some poems! Is that OK with you?" He doesn't do it because he has done hundreds of readings over the years, has read to audiences that have numbered anywhere from one person to three hundred. He has always respected his audience, whatever the turnout, and never gotten angry during readings.

This time he reads seven poems in less than fifteen minutes, a quarter of an hour of hell during which he tries to keep his end of the bargain. Not knowing where the store was, he had shown up earlier in the day to check in with the staff. He noticed on the large bulletin board near the front counter that a woman mystery writer was to be signing at the same time as his scheduled reading that night. He panicked and asked for the person in charge of the signings. When the young man came, the poet asked him if this was the correct night. The kid laughed and said yes. The poet asked him why his name and the name of his new book were not on the bulletin board alongside the mystery writer. The kid did not have an answer and laughed again. The poet told him to write his name and book on the board, waiting as the kid got a marker and scrawled the words in loud orange letters.

Hours later, the high school girl is shuffling friendly expressions on her face, doing her best to make the poet feel good. She has appreciated each of the seven poems, applauding after two of them. The talking man finally leaves right before the poet has decided to quit, walking out of the café without turning to the person standing in front of the mic. As soon as he leaves, his woman friend gets up from her table and enters the bookstore. The poet stops reading and places one hand on the stack of seventeen copies of his book the store ordered for the event. Why not sixteen or eighteen books? Why seventeen?

No one buys a book. Not one single copy. The high school girl is staring at the poet, who waits by the table of books for someone to pick up a copy so he can sign it. She is saved from having to buy one when her boyfriend shows up and leaves the café with her. She does not thank the poet for the reading. This reminds him that he knew it was going to be this kind of evening when he walked in earlier and saw his name missing from the board announcements. He had a gut feeling, but went through with it.

The poet closes his reading copy, picks up his notebook, and turns toward the magazine racks. Outside, a sudden thunder-and-lightning storm sweeps over the area. He spots the kid in charge of the readings holding the front door open for customers running in from the rain. Loud thunder erupts across the mall parking lot as lightning sparks in the distance. The poet takes the side exit into the mall and does not bother to say good-bye to the kid. He walks past several department stores and emerges into the storm. His umbrella is in the car, so the poet half runs and half walks there. He jumps in and looks down at his reading copy and wet clothes. His new book of poems stayed dry during the jog to the car. Despite the long walk to the car, he can't find a drop of water on the book. He holds it closer to his face and stares at the cover. There is not one single stain on the book, so he drives away.

I receive thousands of poems about the moon and don't know what to do. I have this magazine, and it has *moon* in the title, and every famous poet—or every unknown poet—has to send me at least one poem about the moon. I run through the streets of poetry and look up at the orange ball that has left me down here. When the voices know what to say, it says nothing back and makes me feel homeless, a wandering fool with boxes full of poems about the moon. What is left for me? Can they really say what they feel and expect the moon to know? What is it about poets and moons?

Once, when I fell on the sidewalk, I lay there as a little boy and heard drumming in the distance. It was the two kids down the block who hated me and were always pounding on the walls of their house, calling down the moon to punish the quiet ones like me in the neighborhood. I tripped and hurt my knee, so I lay there in pain as their beautiful drumming reached my ears. I looked toward the evening sky, but there was no moon, only the thin dance of clouds that promised I would get home in pain and wait for those boys to get me at school. I receive so many poems about the moon that I am going to become an expert on that special kind of pain. When I am convinced I know everything about the moon, I will fold the magazine and start a new one and call it *Dog*.

Home is where I taped shut a box that is heavy with first editions and multiple copies of some of my books that a stranger sent me almost two months ago. In an e-mail, he asked if I would do him the favor of signing them for him. Like a fool, I said yes, and they quickly arrived weeks ago. I have sat on them since discovering he is a rare-book dealer. After finding that some of the titles he sent me were proof copies, I e-mailed him and got him to admit it. If I signed them, they would increase in value, he would get all the money as a bookseller, and I would not see any royalties. I tell him this on another e-mail and threaten him with signing only the hardcover first editions and paperbacks and shredding the proof copies. He lives in Tuckahoe, New York, a place I have never heard of as he e-mails back and admits he could sell them for profit, but begs me not to destroy the proofs he spent months collecting. It also makes me wonder how much he paid greasy book reviewers who sold him proofs of the latest Gonzalez because there was no way they would review them and their rent was due.

He wanted to know if I could still sign all the books and send them back. I said yes, but inadvertently sat on the stack for weeks, finally signing them, including the proofs, and taping up the box. I come home in a foul mood after the Snyder reading and stare at the box. It has been two months, and the box has been ready to go for a while. I have pasted the man's postage on the outside, and it will not cost me a thing. I get back on the bus when he e-mails me the morning of the Snyder reading to say he can get me a reading at a top-notch poetry festival, famous for bringing only the biggest names to read. He wants to know if I have sent back his books. I have not, but intend to get to the post office right away. I e-mail him to tell him I have gotten as far as taping the box. As a wounded veteran of the po-bizz, I know how these things work and tell him to quit wasting his time promising me things he can't deliver. As of this writing, he is waiting silently for his box. I think about hauling the heavy box of signed books to the post office, adding up how much money he might make.

The following morning I shuffle papers, boxes, and manila files around my cluttered office as I work on various writing projects. Searching for an old folder, I run across copies of *City Pages*, a weekly newspaper from Minneapolis that ran a feature on local poets one year ago. April is National Poetry Month, but you don't want to get me into that because the feature was one of the most ridiculous and superficial things I have ever seen a newspaper do with poetry. The guy who organized it meant well, and he is the editor of an outstanding poetry journal based in Minneapolis, but the newspaper fumbled the feature. They got him to ask us really stupid questions about our lives, our likes and dislikes (bordering on stuff like "What is your favorite color?" etc.), and got each poet to write two poems. There were six poets in the feature, and we were asked to write one poem about a famous landscape in Minnesota and one on a famous Minnesota personality. Opening the newspaper one year later, though it is National Poetry Month again, I have to admit that my poem about rocker Paul Westerberg, former leader of the legendary Replacements, and my poem on crossing the bridge over the Minnesota River aren't so bad for made-to-order verse. I jump back on the poetry ride when I reread the two pieces after forgetting about them for one year.

The other good thing that came out of the *City Pages* joke is that I met a good photographer who was paid to take professional shots of the featured poets. I kept in touch with him, and he provided the back-cover photo for my *Selected Poems*. I spent a year and a half editing it, cutting old poems out, and having nightmares over the ancient poems I left in the selection. Unfortunately, the poem chosen for the bus posters is not included in the book, and its sudden reappearance after thirty years sends paranoid waves through me because I don't know if I have made the right choices for the book.

I have also spent months tracking down back-cover blurbs for my *Selected Poems*, the pressure from my publisher to find known names sending me on a year-long quest. Two good quotes have already come in, but one week after the Snyder reading, I am going in person to ask Robert Bly, the most famous Minnesota poet, to provide the third blurb. He is reading at a library near my home, an event that surprises me because legends rarely trek to the suburbs for readings. He wrote a blurb for one of my earlier books five years ago. I called him on the phone one month ago, but he never answered. Bly is always traveling, and I need to pin him down and get the final blurb.

I have provided fourteen blurbs for other poets' books in the past two years. I get back on the bus each time their publishers take the time to send me a copy when the book comes out, though I receive many anyway as review copies through the book review journal I write for. During those two years of blurbing fourteen books, I have also received approximately six hundred books for review and have not paid one penny for them. I get tons of them in the mail, sent to me by eager and naive publicity staff, through the book review magazine, and from friends and people who seek my blessing. I am pushed off the city transit when I share with friends this tidbit about my writing of blurbs. Yes, a blurb can be seen as some kind of anointing of an author's work. It is also an automatic push of keyboard buttons because it is easy to save your blurbs on your computer, move some words around, and send the latest versions to whomever requests them. The bus takes off without me because this shameful confession reveals the present state of poetry publishing and not—I repeat, not—the present state of the person who was asked to write the blurb. I say this because as someone who has been an editor for twenty-five years, I know how the game works, and those six hundred new books of poetry published over the past two years might contain twenty-three to twenty-four titles worth praising, promoting, and recommending to others. Sure, it comes down to taste, but in twenty-five years of witnessing everything in the po-bizz and piling up requests for blurbs and other acts of anointing, I have seen plenty of poetic vehicles in the garage of metaphor, their wheels ripped off, their sides bashed in, their paint peeling off, and their drivers fired, laid off, or given grants either to go teach lousy workshops to people who can't write or attend writers conferences where famous poets are invited and paid small fortunes to read without having to barter with rare-book dealers who want their signed proof copies returned.

This reminds me of the reading and reception for the Poetry in Motion poster unveiling. One of the deans from the college that hosted the event told the audience she was going to read a haiku from one of the posters, a poem written by a fine local poet who couldn't make it that day. She said she had mistaken him for Jack Kerouac because Kerouac wrote many haikus, and she had wanted to know how the program got permission to use a Kerouac poem as well as an Emily Dickinson. (Don't deans know about public domain?) Everyone in the audience beamed with recognition of Kerouac's name and thought the comparison to the local writer was cute. Another poet and close friend of the haiku's missing author shook her head and whispered to me that she was glad he wasn't there. "I can't wait to e-mail him and tell him he was compared to Kerouac," she said.

Mistaken identity or too many poems? Programs hosted by the wrong people? No, these things have to do with the fact that, despite National Poetry Month every April and calls for a larger audience for poetry, we are drowning in too many poems and too many poets. I never thought I would say that. The dean's brief reference to Kerouac reminded me that I had three poetry contests to judge, and two of the deadlines were coming up fast. I am scrambling because there are too many poets, and they are suffocating themselves in every imaginable contest.

I have judged fifty to sixty poetry contests over the past twenty years—high school, college, literary center competitions, along with serious screening and selection of manuscripts and individual poems for literary journals. I have seen the game play itself out when I recommend winners to final judges, but my screened selections conveniently disappear and are replaced by manuscripts written by the judges' favorite students. Years ago two high school students claimed they wrote the same winning poem. No idea how the West Coast school solved that one. Most of the contests I have judged have been serious and clean, though there are always rumors out there that the judge who selected the winning poem for a big journal actually wrote it under a different name. Of course, the most common underlying gossip has judges selecting their best friends, even for competitions where poems are submitted anonymously. Sure.

For five days in the summer, I am a writer again. This sounds weird for someone who has published a number of books in recent years. For five days, I hide out in a mountain cabin in Caribou, Colorado, and do nothing but write. It is the first time I have done this, and it is overwhelming and very rewarding. Not only do I produce many new poems and dozens of pages of prose, but I immerse myself in a deep isolation that during the week is sometimes hard to take. As a university professor and a professional writer, I have not known this kind of solitude in years. The overpowering landscape around me—that forested mountain wall that rises to the sky and surrounds the cabin on three sides—is amazing in its ability to show me how tiny I am and how its magnetic pull has a great deal to do with days and days of writing.

The first two days go by the quickest because I can't get off the laptop computer I brought with me. Nineteen poems streamed out the first day, and they exhaust me with their sudden arrival. They came from notebooks and are composed on the computer. When my eyes get tired, I sit in one of the study rooms and scribble poem after poem in my notebook. After a lunch break and a nap, I transfer them to the computer. The second day is just as productive, and I start writing short-short essays I have been wanting to do for a long time. The topics vary from recent trips to New Mexico to meditations on being bitten by a spider. I limit each essay to four pages and have fun creating the first drafts. Most of the new poems are finished, but such abundant new prose is going to require a great deal of revision. I have fifteen new short-short essays, but I came here to write, not to worry about perfection. That comes later. By the third day, I am enormously happy about the writing, but the solitude knocks me over the head. I start to get restless and realize I have not been this alone in more than ten years. There is another writer upstairs, but he has a car and comes and goes. I did not rent one. The people who run the retreat are wonderful and make you feel at home, but I go down to the main cabin to talk to them only a few times.

I face my solitude and the draining process of writing and have a brief anxiety attack where I think I'm going to die. What is going on in the midst of a great week of creativity? I move away from my writing table and walk around the room, shut off the computer, and read from books I brought with me. This calms me down, but I start thinking about political problems with individuals at school, about certain relationships with other writers, and about the unfinished tasks I have left at home—including a long-delayed second issue of my poetry magazine. But I came here to write, not to ponder my complicated life in the academic and literary world. I do breathing exercises and feel better, the thoughts of the real world slowly going away. I sit up. This is the real world. I am here on this mountain to write and have nothing else to do here but write. This is my real world this week, and to fight the dominating forces of solitude is self-defeating.

I go with the rhythm of my isolation. I wake up in the middle of the night, wonder if the bears and mountain lions have come down to flip over trash cans outside, and let the problems and events of daily life leave my body. I fall back asleep. Blue jays and woodpeckers keep me company. The distant outlines of mountains to the north change color each time I go out to the porch for a break. I cook for myself all week. There is time for napping, reading, pondering what I have just written, and taking notes in my journals. When was the last time I could do all this in complete privacy? I keep writing, with the morning sessions the most productive. I have been a writer and am grateful for the gift. I feel proud of my pages and pages of rough drafts. I will work on them throughout the summer at home. New material. By the end of the week, I feel stronger, with those moments of fear over encountering this artistic isolation not as frequent.

To retreat must mean to go back. I have gone back to being a writer, and it has been a fun, exhausting, surprising, and sometimes frightening experience. The poems and essays have come from deep within my physical body, my soul, my intellect, and—most important—my life.

A poet steps out and leaves the migraine of several truths behind. He writes as if the poems arrive without sacrifice, knocking them out on the keyboard, amazing himself at how easy this new sequence has given itself to him. The poet steps away from the past and feels uncertain because the fresh poems are about tomorrow, and he doesn't quite know if his eyes are completely open to some things that may happen, though they are already set forth in a number of new pieces. As he flashes the next poem, and then the following long one appears on the screen, he doesn't think about revision, simply wonders where this voice has been and how it came to awaken him during a period when he was starting to question his loyalty to poetry. He was starting to forget his own poems, often depending on the sound of others, which is not destruction, but a temporary notion of survival. A poet steps out and avoids having to confess he doesn't have a clue about the meaning of many of the lines he is printing, the stanzas, long and short, narrow and wide, obscuring their pull on his anxiety—the warmest manner of greeting himself on the page without having to look too deeply into things.

He opens a book of poems by Theodore Roethke, one of the first modern poets he read in his youth, and finds a passage he has not examined in years—"The true point of the spirit sways / Not like a ghostly swan / But as a vine, a tendril / Groping toward a patch of light"—then a later one—"My mind moves in more than one place, / In a country half-land, half-water." He gazes beyond the radiation of the screen and lets go of the newly arrived sequence of poems. He doesn't have to read them closely yet because he isn't there. A poet steps out and abandons what he has discovered because the birth of unknown writing means he has been afraid to get close to it; thus poem after poem has had to borrow details from his life and has formed its own imagination. It is the result of stepping away, creating distance between the quick, though troubled manner in which he writes, escaping the daily air of ideas, and simply casting his fingers over the keyboard in a challenge to his lifelong devotion to the written word—that scribbled line or stanza the pen wove across the white page of bound notebooks. A poet moves away when he releases the handwritten poem and allows the spontaneous one to follow the cursor of electricity across the screen. Perhaps it is like Roethke's mind occupying more than one point in time, existing in various stages of the soul where land and water become one mental landscape that fertilizes what shall be written, labored over, and kept, both publicly and privately. Like Roethke, the poet senses the light is what attaches one poem to the next and the next, each surprising statement, vision, and meditation circling what he has tried to learn from the old master's work. He is always trying to learn, but is too busy writing.

A poet steps out to insist that the mind game of poetic attraction become the mental dance of words whose images and revelations set the stage for grand pronouncements—variations on the dark tendril searching for illumination that must show itself before the poet can stop composing and reexamine what he has done. The poet stands aside when the stack of printed poems sit quietly on his desk because their passage through the printer is an early signal that their grand pronouncements will be diminished by the world and his readership, which rarely allow such a huge focus and understanding of human chaos. Set in the neat stack of white paper, the poems become themselves—daily habit and mutterings stripped of philosophy in order to retain the rapture, keep their whole, and find a way to survive in narrower acceptance.

A poet bounces back when Roethke also writes, "In the long journey out of the self, / There are many detours, washed out interrupted raw places." It is an interruption to have a large number of new poems. It is a change, a dance, the surprise of solitude and devotion that might punish the poet by allowing longer time and distance between its rushes and pourings. The detours must not be moved aside because they are mightier than the screen that invites poem after poem, flash draft after flash draft that lives and dies behind the cursor, their brief shaping and evolution witnessed only by their creator, who washes out the invisible words and erased visions because they do not belong there. They have accidentally arrived in the intensity of sequence because the poet who steps out does not completely understand himself, and his need to control the language is actually an example of lack of control. Yet how much do the raw places carry in value and weight when the eyes of an anonymous readership will place their own interruptions on the poet's work once it is in their few hands?

A poets steps out as the manuscript grows, and he recalls what Robert Frost said: "If a book of poems contains twenty-four poems, the book is the twenty-fifth." But what does the poet who is stepping away know about books? Yes, it is a sequence that may lead to a book, but it is also his life, and it is why he is stepping outside of his ingrained identity. He is busy in thoughts of suggestion and surprise, lost in moments of becoming more aware of himself as a writer—those seconds when familiarity is a punishing, sober wave of fulfillment. A poet steps out in time to silence the sound of speech, allowing it to lie in the gravel of his old notebooks—their yellowing pages a reminder of yesterday and a gift granted the poet who is not afraid to step back—before catching the low hum of technology that might trust the heart as it gets out of the way to let the poet step through.

There is no such thing as anonymity in the po-bizz, and I can't help but jump back on the blue bus when I hear how one local poetry editor is publishing his former teachers, current friends, and hangers-on who make up one of the most active groups of literary producers in Minneapolis. I jump back on because what I observe tells me my theories are correct and what I have done with my poetry career must be worth something to somebody, someday. In a world where there are too many poets, it is easier to publish your friends and get the fat foundation grants because you have a track record to show the funders. It doesn't matter that some insiders know how phony your editorial tastes are and how much you cheapen your product by taking the mongoloid approach to poetry—publish your incestuous, inner circle because it strengthens and reinforces the wagons you have circled against the rest of the po-bizz world!

This brings up a dilemma I have found among a number of young poets, an issue I have wrestled with off and on for decades. If there are too many poets out there as you are starting out, and you have knowledge of how nasty and incestuous the scene can be, do you write to get published, or do you write to be yourself and worry later about publishing? It is a tough question. I have talked to many poets who have experienced this odd feeling—"I am writing new poems because they might fit this journal I want to get into, although they have rejected my normal style before. I am writing new poems because such-and-such magazine is looking for this kind of poems, and it is a prolific time for me, and I am producing work I will dash off to the journal as soon as I can print out the poems!"

It happens all the time, and many young poets take care of this pressure by doing exactly that—writing to get published, working poems together to fit into certain dominant schools of the po-bizz and to increase their chances of being noticed and added to the flooded community of poets, a bursting world where very few poets, regardless of their age or how many books they have published, ever enjoy the simple pleasure of having one of their poems reproduced on a beautiful poster for public viewing. It doesn't matter to me how many thousands of riders on Minneapolis's buses glance at my poem without reading it or comprehending it as they search for a seat during a crowded rush hour. The fact is that my poem is up there in public view, and to be in the public eye in an artistically professional manner is very, very rare in the po-bizz these days. It is why I bathed in the pure enjoyment of the Poetry in Motion project—it was a chance to have my poem recognized and to place greater distance between me and the horrors of the po-bizz world that swirl around me and that have been spinning faster as each decade of too many poets increases in velocity.

Plus, I haven't even talked about rejection. This subject is a whole different essay where I can tell you about my twenty-five years as an editor who has been physically threatened by poets I rejected, sent photocopies of hands flipping the bird at me for turning down their poems, sent sexual offers in trade for publication, and had hundreds—literally hundreds—of rejected poets respond to rejection in every possible psychopathic manner. Plus, plus—yes, a second *plus*—I haven't written about the dozen or so poets whose work I have accepted and who have also reacted in a hostile manner either because I took three of their poems instead of five or because their number one enemy appeared on page 12 of my anthology, but they only made it onto page 150.

You think the idea of too many poets is elitist, don't you? Well, tell that to the U.S. poet laureates who have hit the public stage over the past few decades with the common cry for more poems with a "reader-friendly" character to them. I picked that phrase off the latest anthology published by a former poet laureate, the second volume in a series he is doing for a major New York publisher as part of his contribution to expanding the audience for poetry. During his notorious reign as poet laureate, he constantly repeated the idea of "reader-friendly" poems to the packed audiences that flocked to his readings. According to an insider friend, he echoed this theme to the one thousand people who waited for him in Chicago a few years ago. They squirmed in the rows of tightly packed seats inside an ancient auditorium because the poet laureate was late, again. When he finally showed up, almost one hour after the scheduled time to read, he stumbled down a flight of stairs because he was sloshed, drunk to high heaven as he verified the rumors that preceded his name, though my friend claims he shocked everyone by getting up off the floor and giving a great reading that got his loyal following to forget right away about his demons. Reader-friendly poetry won out that night, and the man sold hundreds of books. I wonder what kind of fumes were given off at the signing table—reader-friendly or unfriendly?

Ah, U.S. poets laureate! One of my favorite topics of the po-bizz! I imagine myself stamping my feet on the empty bus parked in front of the Poetry in Motion college because I want to shake the driver and the blonde bureaucrat to wake up to the reader-friendly poems they have been forced to display on their clean bus. Instead, I sit in my home office, shove the sealed box of my signed books under my desk, and reread my review of two books by the newest poet laureate, an old friend from my Denver days who is the first U.S. poet laureate to bring dignity to the position. I state this opinion in the article several times and reread one of my favorite passages from my review:

> For more than a decade, well-connected figures from privileged and powerful poetry circles stepped forward to proclaim their commitment to enlarging the audience for poetry by getting out there to be "the people's poet." This was a laughable masquerade because the chosen bards would have to go against their cynical natures, lay down their elitist approaches to poetic form, and pay attention to people who wrote differently than they did, people who were not published by a poetry establishment that called the shots as to who was in and who was out of the butcher shop. Previous holders of the position would rather give up their academic endowments than their membership in the boys' club!

I howl as I reread this passage for the hundredth time. I am howling (Snyder mentioned Allen Ginsberg's legendary poem "Howl" the other night) because the new poet laureate loved my review and ordered hundreds of copies of the issue from the magazine's office in Denver. I scream because the Library of Congress, the official sponsor of the poet laureate position, weighs in by ordering two hundred copies of the issue. I am in tears of laughter as I wonder what they will say when they read the passage I just quoted. To top off this hit issue of an annual poetry feature I edit for the magazine, I get a personal, handwritten letter from Jim Harrison, one of my favorite writers. It arrives along with the latest two-ton box of review copies from Denver. Harrison loves my review! One of my heroes acknowledges me and says that the new poet laureate, an old friend of his, called him up and read him the review in the middle of the night. They did the male thing over the phone and loved it, celebrating my nerve to tell it like it is.

Nerve? Hell, no. It's poetry, and I have to get myself to put that box of signed books in the mail today because I am almost done with my bus ride. But I instead go to the second reading by a legendary poet in one week. What a life! I have to get the poet to do a blurb for my book, but the tiny room in the suburban library is packed, and the Minnesota hero is getting old, though he is on tonight. Unlike at disappointing readings of the past few years, he is hot and on the ball tonight, working his cult audience with a fiery presence. Instead of the dragging old fart I've heard in recent readings, he is hyper and does a great reading. About 150 people are packed into the small room, though I get there early and sit in the front row. A couple of seats down is an old woman, maybe late eighties, with her daughter who lives nearby, and the old woman came from Madison, Minnesota, the poet's hometown, for the reading. I hear her tell a man next to me that she is the poet's old neighbor and was one of his first typists in the early days when he used to live in an old cabin and wrote inside his chicken coop in Madison. The poet has not seen her in years and gives her a hug. He spots me right away and shakes my hand and asks why I came so far to hear him. I tell him I live only eight miles down the road. He tells the audience it is his first time in Eagan, which is a southern suburb south of the airport. Someone in the audience yells out that the governor is from there, and the icon says he is going home.

He walks into the library with a grocery bag full of an Ally Press book of poems on Iraq, a book I reviewed in the Denver publication. He pulls out stacks of them and starts throwing them at the crowd, hitting people on the head until many of them come up and take them because he says he is giving them all out for free. Right before he starts, he throws me a new book of his poems that Eastern Washington University Press just published, short poems like those in *Silence of the Snowy Fields*, his first book of forty years ago, wonderful poems different from his recent *ghazals*. He says they are Madison poems and he received ten copies in the mail that day. He reads the Iraq stuff, rips on George Bush, then reads from his anthology of translations. After reading his usual suspects like Mirabai and Kabir, he asks if anyone has a request.

I yell, "Machado!" He says, "Antonio! No one called him Machado!" and reads about five incredible poems by the great Spanish poet, calling him Machado the rest of the evening. Then he reads a few poems from the

Eastern Washington book before finishing with two poems from a forth-coming HarperCollins book. I have the proofs, but won't be selling them to any book dealer. Of course, a huge line of followers forms after the reading, stacks of books to be signed heavy in the suburban dwellers arms.

I am tired and do not want to wait in line to ask the man for a blurb. I will call him on the phone again and keep trying until I get my blurb. After all, Robert Bly is Robert Bly, so I drive my car home in the rain, thoughts of staying on the bus and getting the elusive blurb lost in my enjoyment of his reading.

It has stopped raining today, and I have some contest deadlines to meet, along with a huge pile of new poetry books to review for the next issue of the Denver journal. In my haste over these tasks, I swear I have stumbled twice over the unmailed box of my signed books. My wife and I have already selected the frame for the poster we will mount in the foyer of our home. The coordinator of the Poetry in Motion project told us the ink on the posters is still wet, so we have to wait for our set to arrive in the mail. I spend the time fingering the bookmarks, making lists in my head of who deserves one in a rare snail mail and who might get an actual poster I am very proud of. I repeat my pride because the audience at the poster unveiling truly enjoyed our brief reading and had many good things to say about all six posters. I can't wait to look at mine hanging in the foyer each morning as I venture forth to excavate a new place in the po-bizz after one year of sabbatical, one year of writing and pondering the shifting bus routes of poetic musings. One of the last things I saw at the community college as I left the unveiling was the blond woman getting off the poetry bus after the cop left. He let the two kids go and ignored the Jesus freak with the flying pamphlets. I walked to my car as the blond Metro Transit employee unclipped a poetry bookmark off her clipboard and handed it to the religious man who was still trying to keep his pamphlets on the table. I was too far down the sidewalk to identify which bookmark she handed the man, though I swear, as I crossed the busy intersection to the parking garage, I saw the Jesus man let the poem launch itself out of his hands and into the powerful winds of the city.

Part Four

A Break with the Past

I drive around aimlessly in my hometown because my hometown is gone. El Paso is no longer the city I grew up in—this statement is one of the most common and initial perceptions anyone who returns home usually has, whether it is expressed to others or left in the mind of the native who has been gone a long time. As I drive through the neighborhoods of my childhood and count the number of houses that are decaying, I recall how new they looked when I was a kid. As I pause at a four-way stop and there are no other cars waiting to proceed, I realize that digging into El Paso's past will not bring it back to my satisfaction. It is too late, and the National Guard will be here soon to pretend they can seal the invisible border between my hometown and Mexico, a boundary line that has been as transparent as my need to flee the area in 1978. As I wander through a city I still love and can't tell myself all the reasons why, I search for who-knows-what in a metropolis that is constantly re-creating itself in a politically volatile region.

According to critic Samuel Truett, writing in the summer 2004 issue of the *Journal of the Southwest*, the word *desert* comes from the Latin verb *deserere*, which means "to sever connection with." This makes me conclude that El Paso, as a city, may no longer be mine, but it is difficult to feel I have lost all connections with the desert itself. Perhaps the natural landscape of the Rio Grande, the Franklin Mountains, and the Chihuahua Desert now belong to some other native son who carries a different version of life in the old border town. This person sees things I can't see each time he comes home to visit. Since El Paso may no longer be mine, I find myself driving around calmly, no longer the inquisitive writer in search of the grand find—the overlooked historic detail that may tie the fractured bilingual present to the past. I drive up and down Mesa, Paisano, and Alameda, major thoroughfares that have given me many ideas on what to write about, and am no longer afraid I will miss something or come upon some forgotten detail from my past that will unlock some of the reasons why I keep coming back. Contradictions? Anyone who lives in this region is full of contradictions over lifestyle, the economy, language, politics, and that ever-present, though always invisible U.S.–Mexican border over which Americans throughout the country are now fighting. Of course, the majority of them have never been to the area, would never dream of living here, and know practically nothing about southwestern culture. This vacuum can be depressing when you take the fate of millions of citizens and undocumented workers into account, but this national ignorance of the place where I grew up no longer brings back the old sadness I used to carry with me each time I came home to visit from years of living in other parts of the United States. The sadness is gone because I have given up my claim on El Paso. Its larger, younger, and nonnative population—the majority of those people moving to the desert from elsewhere—can have it because I don't recognize it any longer, and the stationing of National Guard troops along the Rio Grande will be the final action that will sever my old El Paso from the new one with its perilous future. What has changed within me to remove the old fear of the city, the desert, and the unpredictable border? I drive around and look in peace, but what I find is often different than what I used to seek. Perhaps it comes down to growing older and finally being able to visit with tranquility. Age and time do this. What happened to the passion for exploration—the need to dig in the desert sand and write about its hidden history?

A big surprise is 2006 data showing that El Paso's crime rate is one of the lowest in the country. This information is shocking to many of its citizens, whose houses are reinforced with bars on their windows and doors, and to those who have been victims of a notoriously high rate of car theft. Of course, the four hundred unsolved murders of women in Juárez and the continuing violence between drug cartels in northern Mexico are not included in the statistics because they take place in Mexico, right across the river. Yet border violence and life-threatening dramas play themselves out along its waters every single day. What has happened to reduce El Paso's crime rate? Are the police doing a better job? Recent statistics also list at least two hundred youth gangs spread throughout the city. Sunland Park Mall, near my mother's house, was consistently in the news throughout the summers of 2003 and 2004 because of the high number of carjackings in the parking lot. Some thieves, tired of working so late at night, must have decided it was easier simply to drag drivers out of their vehicles during the day or to demand their keys as they walked out of the mall, their arms loaded with shopping bags.

I have a silly theory about the reduced crime wave, and it is tested when I have dinner with my three sisters and their families at a posh Mexican restaurant. As we order the food, one of my sisters reveals that all three of them saw Mel Gibson's film *The Passion of the Christ* when it came out a couple of years ago. I am sipping on my glass of water and start to choke when my youngest sister, who is sitting across from me at the long table, tells me what a wonderful film it is and her husband nods in agreement. My second-oldest sister overhears our conversation and agrees about how emotional it was to see Gibson's controversial and bloody rendition of Christ's final, agonizing days on earth. I keep choking as I realize they have bought the radical, conservative view of the film and have forgotten how I feel about right-wing, fundamentalist movements that insist each believer stop breathing and start swallowing their brand of blind faith. We were raised Catholic, but my family quit going to church decades ago. My sisters and brothers-in-law are not necessarily acting like fundamentalists, but it is shocking and revealing how the visual imagery Gibson manipulated has hypnotized millions into believing this is it—the coming of the Christ we have been waiting for.

I calm down and announce, "The movie is nothing but right-wing propaganda!" This statement creates a chilly silence across the table, until a couple of my sisters whisper to each other about what I said and one of them changes the topic. My theory on the crime data is that many El Pasoans are being tamed by things like Gibson's film and the many new churches I see sprouting all over the previously empty desert. More religion might equal less crime, and I have never seen so many new places to worship in the old hometown. El Paso is starting to remind me of the Midwest, where I live and can count a Lutheran or Catholic church on every other street corner. The traditional Mexican, Roman Catholic way in which my family was raised has been being erased and replaced with the easy availability of Gibson's hard-hitting, anti-Semitic, visual message. A good portion of young Mexican Americans in El Paso do not go to church, and many who do are not Catholics automatically. Millions have reacted to the film since its release; fundamentalist churches are buying the DVD by the thousands; and my sisters have bought into the marriage between media and faith—not necessarily a new development in a conservative society, but certainly something that changes the dynamics in a border region that has been traditionally Catholic, though many will argue that Mexican Catholicism, with its high level of intolerance, is not any different from the powerful waves of Christian fundamentalism flooding the country, even El Paso. My sisters and I had a nice dinner anyway. I have not seen the film and don't plan to see it. Mel Gibson and the surprises over the latest crime data add to the changing hometown landscape. Maybe more people are attending church in El Paso or at least buying *The Passion of Christ* on DVD and converting traditional border aggression into passion in the desert.

A few streets that no longer exist in El Paso: Martinez, Hammitt, Pera, Lata, Miranda, Boone, Castillo, Obregon, Sala, Mitchell, and Pintero. Most of them were torn up to build the first freeway in 1959. The others were swallowed by city growth and new buildings, all of them located in east El Paso, not far from El Calvario Catholic Church, an old landmark of the barrio in that area.

Some of the last things that happened on these streets:

April 12, 1958: Two drunks crash their car into a stone wall on Martinez. Both men are decapitated in the wreck, the one named Alfredo Vasquez a notorious marijuana smuggler who died with one thousand dollars in his pockets, five pounds of the weed spilling all over Martinez, seeding the dirt around the asphalt a few weeks before it was torn up by busy tractors.

May 10, 1958: A naked woman ran down Hammitt street screaming something about a man dressed completely in black trying to break into her house. Being used to the wild happenings in her home, her neighbors ignored her until they heard sirens from the fire engines and came out into the night to watch the woman's house go up in flames. They never saw Leticia Santiago again. Two weeks later her entire block was razed, Leticia having been one of the last residents to defy the city's plans for a freeway.

June 8, 1958: Strange markings in white chalk appeared one morning on Pera Street. People came out of their houses to look at the stick figures dancing around a circle. They blamed it on Arturo, the neighborhood mental case, but Arturo was back in the nut ward at Thompson General Hospital. The drawings were rather intricate and included eagles, deer, lizards, and the outlines of saguaros—a cactus unknown in the Chihuahua Desert. The various animals encircled what looked like the stick figure of a man kneeling in front of a candle. The entire set of drawings spanned about twenty yards. No one had seen anything like it, and the *El Paso Herald Post* even sent a reporter and photographer to investigate and take pictures. As the summer heat of the day intensified, the chalk drawings began to disappear, leaving the residents to wait for the newspaper people. By the time the news team showed up, the images had totally faded from the steaming pavement. The reporter looked at the few remaining neighbors like they were crazy when they tried to describe what they saw. Pera was one of the last streets torn apart in the area.

August 17, 1958: A couple of World War II veterans, Alfonso Mora and Ricardo Sanchez, knifed each other to death on Lata Street. Witnesses swear the men embraced each other in a death grip as they fell on the bloody sidewalk. When police arrived almost one hour later—murders in the Lata neighborhood not being top priority for the El Paso Police Department at the time—officers found the two bodies with their heads missing. Neighbors hid behind closed doors, a few venturing out to tell police that the bodies were intact when they fell. The newspaper account of the strange deaths did not mention the missing heads, though Ramiro Marquez, an *El Paso Times* reporter in the early 1960s, heard about the men, investigated, and was told accounts of police taking away the two headless bodies in the coroner's truck. City records show no autopsies, and Marquez was unable to get officials to dig up the bodies at Fort Bliss cemetery to check on the rumors about headless drunks and old war buddies doing themselves in.

October 23, 1958: Miranda Street. My drunk great-uncle Jose, fresh from getting out of the city jail, is almost run down by a late-night taxi cab as he staggers across Miranda, trying to find his way home to my grandmother Julia's house. His sister has tolerated his bouts before, though they always come at a price if he arrives when she is asleep. This night is different because Jose can't find the right street and winds up passing out near the doors to Tencho's Bar, a place he is banned from for fighting with customers. The police cruiser finds him, and off to jail he goes again. It will be the last time Jose passes out on that street because he vanishes from El Paso a few weeks later and is never heard from again by anyone in my family.

November 2, 1959: Pintero Street. Four Mexican women in the South El Paso community known as Little Chihuahua either claimed to be or were exposed as *brujas* (witches) by some of their very strict Catholic neighbors. The women were popular with some of their neighbors, who depended on them for remedial cures and herbal remedies. They frightened other people with their unusual habits. Lucha Contreras, age fifty-six, loved to show her tattooed breasts to any man who walked by her apartment door. She was known for her wild cries in the middle of the night and the way drunk men would come to see her and always leave sober. Maria Ramirez, age sixty-two, lived in a tiny house filled with dozens of glass jars full of unusual herbs, dried plants, lizard and snake bones, crushed grasshoppers and ants, and other unidentifiable ingredients. She was famous for having given birth to stillborn twins whose webbed feet would have given them trouble if they had lived. Maria Velasquez, age eighty-nine, was the oldest of the group and was locally famous for having claimed she was Pancho Villa's abortionist. In other words, she took care of any problems the legendary general's various mistresses might have had when they violated his orders that the Villa bloodline would not continue in the United States, but in Mexico only. Finally, Dolores Madresca, age seventy-four, whose specialty was healing neighborhood children of any illness by dunking their entire bodies in a deep tin tub she kept in her backyard. Parents who brought their sick child to Dolores were guaranteed a cure in the dark tub water that she filled with secret herbs and things, though the parents had to leave the children and return for them after Dolores was done. People were used to the children screaming in her backyard and recognized the cries as part of the cure. They loved her because whatever was wrong with the boys and girls was gone by the next day, whether it was a fever or the flu or even chicken pox. Her practice came to an end when a doubtful parent, having brought her five-year-old boy Lencho to Dolores for the first time, returned during the ritual to find two huge iguana lizards swimming in the tub with her son, who was in the throes of screaming his lungs out. The mother pulled Lencho away and ran home with the dripping, hysterical boy. The last thing she saw was the crazy woman hugging the lizards to her chest as she pushed them into their wire cages. Three days later Dolores quietly died of a heart attack in her sleep and was found by another neighbor who had knocked and knocked on her door, her eleven-month-old baby girl sweating from a high fever.

December 16, 1958: Boone. I am six years old and walk home with my two cousins, Blanca and Benny, from the bus stop, the three of us having gotten off at the corner of Boone and Alameda, the closest stop for the bus we ride each day from St. Mary's Catholic School near downtown El Paso. Rumors of the witches are floating among the nervous nuns who run the school. I am too young to figure out what these women have done and why my hooded teachers are so upset about them. After all, the neighborhood where they live is a good ten miles away from the school. I ask my older cousin Blanca about the witches. She is in the third grade, and I am in kindergarten. She slaps me across the back of the head and tells me to shut up as we pass El Calvario Catholic Church, where the three of us were baptized. It is the last time we pass the old stone church because school is out for the Christmas holidays and the church will be torn down a couple of weeks after holiday mass because the massive freeway project is about to rip through my childhood.

The church of San José de Concordia de Alto was built in 1850 by the Reverend Ramón Ortíz, curate of the Juárez mission called La Virgen de Guadalupe. San José became the first church built in El Paso, though the area was called Concordia at the time. In May 1932, a tombstone was discovered near the entrance of where the church used to be, excavation of the marker taking place in the center of Concordia cemetery, now the oldest cemetery in El Paso. The tombstone, considered to be the first ever in the mid-nineteenth-century settlement, reads, "Maria Juana Ascarate de Stephenson. Born February 8, 1800. Died February 5, 1857." The stone still stands.

In November 2004 during a Thanksgiving trip home, I visit with Peter Ashkenaz, a lifelong friend. We grew up together in El Paso, and he now lives in Washington, D.C. Along with Marissa, his daughter, we drive around the eastern part of the city, gazing at neighborhoods we have not seen in years and wind up at Concordia. Peter drives the car through a narrow entrance in the high stone fence and parks near the Jewish family plots. We get out of the car, and he takes his daughter and me to his mother's grave. She passed away five years ago, and I was unable to attend the funeral. I did not know she was buried in historic Concordia. I stand in silence near her grave marker as Peter picks a small rock off the ground and sets it calmly on the tombstone. Marissa and I do the same thing without a word, though Peter explains that placing a stone on the grave is an honorable replacement for not bringing fresh flowers. He knows the cemetery well and drives past John Wesley Hardin's grave, which was rediscovered a few years ago and is now surrounded by decorative metal bars and a plaque. The legendary outlaw is back. A sign in the middle of several ancient markers lists some of the other famous people buried at Concordia, including Pascual Orozco, a Mexican politician who fought in the Mexican Revolution and almost became president of Mexico, his forces capturing Juárez several times during the ten years of fighting, most of those years made famous by Pancho Villa, who used El Paso as one of his sanctuaries during the revolution.

In 2004, when Arizona vigilante ranchers shot and killed two undocumented "aliens" from Mexico, the bodies were left in the desert for three days, dozens of vultures hurtling toward the sky in a black cloud, their screams echoing across the canyon as the Border Patrol vans finally pulled up. Three years later, in addition to finding several hundred dead Mexicans who never made it through the 110-degree summer heat of the border, agents came across dozens of abandoned bicycles. The deserts of Arizona, New Mexico, and West Texas are being littered with broken-down bikes that many undocumented people use to get across the deserts faster. Many of the bikes have flat tires because they weren't built to make it across hundreds of miles of rough terrain. Data is showing that the unfortunate Mexicans who die in the middle of nowhere are usually walkers, crossing on foot being the traditional means of trying to find a new life in the United States. The Border Patrol has not found any dead near piles of useless bikes, though their riders could have succumbed later. People wanting to get into the country will try just about anything, but the idea of more bikes being used must carry a deeper metaphor about entry, escape, and departure. One other common item many officers find in the path of so many fleeing people is the rosary. A friend who used to work at one of the El Paso processing centers for undocumented workers claims there are drawers and boxes full of rosaries in one of their storerooms.

There is a Texas state law that has made it illegal to put graffiti on someone else's cow.

In 1531, the first apparitions of la Virgen de Guadalupe appeared to Juan Diego, an Indian in Mexico City. This happened ten years after Hernán Cortés and his soldiers conquered and destroyed the Aztec Empire. In 1541, Franciscan and early historian Motolina of New Spain wrote to the Crown in Madrid that some nine million Aztecs had been successfully converted to Christianity.

One day during the catechism class in which my parents enrolled me to prepare for my first holy communion, a girl in the back of the classroom lifted her skirt and showed me her yellow panties. About half an hour later, a quiet boy who always sat next to me and refused to tell me his name picked his nose and showed me his finger before rubbing it on the back cover of his Bible. When I participated in my first confession, I made up a few sins as I whispered to the priest who sat on the other side of the screen. I intentionally left many of my sins out of the confession. When I went through the ritual of communion and receiving the wafer, I walked quickly to my seat where the rest of the class was kneeling and praying. I couldn't hold back any longer, the line of kids having been long, and I pissed in my pants. I motioned to my mother in tears. She got up from her seat a few rows back and took me out of the pew by the hand, hurrying me home to change. I wore black dress pants, which helped cover what I had done, but couldn't forget the smell in the midst of a bunch of young kids kneeling and praying in their first moments of purity.

Directly across the border from Laredo, Texas, six drug dealers raped the daughter of the local police chief, then hustled several shipments of cocaine across the river. Three days later, two of the dealers were gunned down by Laredo police, one of the dead related to a member of the annual George Washington Celebration committee, who plan one of the largest patriotic events in South Texas, in which thousands of Hispanics celebrate their American citizenship, the men dressing up as Washington and the women as his wife, Martha.

According to one Texas geographer, digging straight down from Austin, the state capitol, will not get you to China, but to Iraq.

The poets saw the Marfa lights and were touched. They wrote poems about the mysterious lights in the mountains of southwestern Texas and how the centuries-old legacy, passed down from Indian to pioneer to Marfa Web site, gave them a true understanding of life in the desert. They decided that the mysteries of Texas were meant to be written about by poets from Boston, Chicago, and Hawaii, the three of them having traveled there as a result of generous fellowships awarded to them by a foundation in Santa Fe and now including their Marfa poems in their newest books published by big-time poetry presses. There is nothing like poets traveling to a foreign landscape and acting like they are qualified to write about its mysteries.

All my best friends in elementary school were Jewish because my neighborhood was in one of the newest suburbs in El Paso during the early 1960s, when Jews with money built homes in that part of town. This was an example of early flight to the suburbs by white people to avoid the reality of downtown El Paso and its encroaching barrios. How we could afford to move to that part of town I will never know since my father was a used-car salesman and never made much money. My Jewish friends hated Catholics and always made jokes about Jesus. They didn't know that I didn't care because the priests, nuns, crucifixes, rosaries, confessional booths, and sheer terror of sinning twenty-four hours a day made me immune to Jesus humor.

Juan Diego died in 1548. In 1555, the second archbishop of Mexico, Alonso de Montfar, indirectly approved the 1531 apparitions of la Virgen de Guadalupe, who wasn't chosen as the patroness of Mexico City until 1737. In 1921, a bomb placed beneath an image of la Virgen in a church in Mexico City exploded, causing great damage, but nothing happened to the image. Not a single damaging mark was found on it. The year 1929 marked the first documented note of an apparent reflected image of a man's head in the right eye of la Virgen, part of a photograph taken by Alfonso Marcue.

By paying a $150 fee, you can become a licensed dead animal hauler in Texas.

From the *Las Vegas Sun*, December 12, 2004:

> A 31-year-old Las Vegas man found at the airport with lizards in his underwear was fined $500 and sentenced to three years of probation for smuggling. Don D. Andrews, an auto detailer and reptile collector, offered no explanation before or after sentencing on Friday after being found with nine dead and three live lizards in his crotch at McCarran International Airport. Two of the lizards were monitors—a Federally protected species. Andrews was arrested at the airport by a Las Vegas detective who testified he became suspicious about the strange bulges in Andrew's crotch. A voluntary search turned up twelve young lizards and an egg wrapped in tube socks. The longest of the reptiles was twelve inches. The three that survived the plane trip later died. Andrews said he bought the lizards in the Philippines from two young priests from one of the largest Catholic churches in the area. Officials on the islands were investigating rumors of a lucrative business in reptile smuggling at the church.

In Odessa, Texas, the Star of David and the peace symbol are forbidden by the city's dress code because they are considered to be Satanic symbols.

In Texas, it's legal for a chicken to have sex with a human, but it's illegal for the human to reciprocate.

A Texas state law forbids people from carrying around a wire cutter or a pair of pliers that could cut a fence.

The last time I went to church as a boy, my father and I had to leave early because I started to faint from the incense fumes the priest kept waving in a smoking cup, a ritual I had never seen before. My father helped me down the long rows of pews, hundreds of worshipers looking up at the boy who almost passed out as he tried to focus on their many faces, one or two women in scarves quickly making the sign of the cross as we stumbled past them.

We know them and carry them with us our entire lives. Even when they appear in our memories, we don't want to think about them. The deepest family secret is humming a song we have refused to sing. When we hear it, we turn away and pretend we don't know the lyrics. That deep secret destroys the future, rearranging it to appear like the past. As we hide the secret over the decades, the impact of our hiding emerges as something we chose to do over something else. When we act, the hellos and good-byes are false because the secret has transformed what we think of one another. When we hold a reunion, there are several clues accidentally left in the open for a few family members to notice, the details reminding them that certain things have remained secret for too long. What goes unsaid forms the shape of the secret, the words not chosen or the experiences never recounted again residing as restless ghosts in the minds of more than one sibling. Things that are said clearly, even repeated, drape a subtle drama over the hidden core. When an unexpected death in the family takes place, the secret takes on a whole new meaning. At the funeral, someone wants to bring up the secret, but is held back by a brother and two sisters. The ones who have never known the secret pay their respects. The ones who carry underground knowledge also pay their respects. When the surviving family members part, promising to visit with one another more often, the deepest secret is buried with the dead relative, the details descending with the casket, the outcome of such actions unclear until the grandchildren, too young to understand adult grief, grow up and secretly take over the family secret.

This does not mean that what I am saying about El Paso is not there. Paper, silence, stone. It does not qualify as truth or false dawn, simply as experience. Tortilla, moustache, pigeon. This does not accent the way it was, but perhaps how it should have been before someone stepped in and changed the way it happened and transformed the hometown into a mutation of what I knew as a child. Opinion, vision, dance. El Paso's decaying infrastructure pronounces its value before the eye and the soul of one who is willing to accept it. The jalapeño rolls off the belly, but this does not mean that it lies behind the biting, piece by piece. Holster, heat, humiliation.

No one stares at portraits of Catholic saints any longer. Those images were buried with the last ancestor who rose from the dead to steal the halo off your head. This does not conclude that the night is faithful and the night is going to prosper. It decides only that Interstate 10 somehow surrounds everything I am writing about, and the mountains, for a change, are not a part of this.

In 1921, at the age of twenty-one, my grandfather Bonifacio noticed a beautiful young girl in the El Paso neighborhood where they both lived. He did not know who the girl was or that she was seventeen years old. Julia's father had passed away in Juárez a few years earlier, and her mother ran off with another man. She and the other man worked in the "campo" outside of Juárez and rode the train each day to work, and she often brought her daughter with her. Bonifacio first spotted Julia in the train yard and tried to think of ways to meet her because, for him, it was love at first sight. He started leaving love notes to this girl in the wheels of the train. Somehow, someone told Julia that a young stranger was leaving notes for her, but she never responded. Bonifacio spent weeks riding his bicycle around central El Paso because he heard the girl's family had moved to Copia Street in that area. He vowed to his aunt that he would find this girl he had fallen in love with. Finally, one day he spotted Julia carrying water in a bucket. She walked alongside her older sister, Lenor. Bonifacio pulled up, jumped off his bike, and told Julia how he felt and convinced her on the spot to run away with him, which is exactly what Julia did. Bonifacio got an old woman friend of his family to keep Julia for a few days until he could finalize plans to leave El Paso with her. The old woman kept telling the seventeen-year-old to go home to her mother, but Julia said she couldn't because her mother would kill her. The next day she and Bonifacio left for Aztec, Arizona, where they lived for a few years. They did not get married until 1927, in Los Angeles, California, where Bonifacio's car was stolen during the wedding trip, forcing them to take the train back to Arizona.

I cross Texas Street in downtown El Paso and pass a bus stop where a giant Aztec calendar has been erected as an attractive marker for tourists. The empty sidewalk and concrete benches are covered with pigeon droppings, and several of the birds mutter and skip out of my way as I cross the street again. The lone sign near the stone calendar says "Feeding the Birds Is Prohibited." No one is feeding them as I head for South El Paso Street in search of the old Roma Hotel, where Pancho Villa loved to stay when he hid in El Paso from his enemies across the river. The hotel used to sit at 419 South El Paso Street, but when I get there, I find the building has been partitioned into storefronts, pawnshops, and used-clothing stores. It is what I expected, of course, but have dreamed of this place because it is near the block where Mexican movie houses were located, and one of them, El Colón Theatre, is key to my search. My dream includes walking up ancient stairs with my grandfather, Bonifacio, whom I never knew, and encountering Villa at the top of the banister from where he threw a German man down the stairs after the stranger insisted on Villa's helping Germany set up submarine and refueling bases on the coast of Mexico. It was 1911, and Villa refused, tossed the man out, and returned to the Elite Confectionary, the ice cream shop next to the hotel, where Villa drank bottle after bottle of strawberry pop. Villa was a great eater and liked candy and sodas in large supply.

I want to find the hotel room where Villa kept his homing pigeons, cages of birds he used to send and retrieve messages between him and his generals in Juárez. I wish I could hear them cooing above the low whir of the fans that Joaquin, Villa's twenty-year-old assistant, kept turned on in the heat of an El Paso summer. Known only by the name "Joaquin," the young man was loved like a son by Villa and remained loyal to him during the early years of the revolution. The general's *mozo* (errand boy) supposedly vanished during the first battle of Juárez, which took place in early May 1911. I have written elsewhere about Bonifacio, my grandfather, also disappearing during that battle, escaping Villa's troops who were rounding up young men to reinforce their numbers in the bloody Juárez encounter between Villa and the Mexican Federal Army.

The Roma Hotel is gone, and downtown El Paso is surprisingly absent of birds—surprisingly because huge flocks of pigeons in San Jacinto Plaza, a few blocks north, are one of my oldest memories of childhood. The only message they carry now comes from a distant memory that keeps me on South El Paso Street because El Colón Theatre has also vanished. I walk past the old site of the Roma and cross another street, sensing I am on the block where El Colón used to stand. I find more clothing stores and a Mexican café in its place, but no theater. I am unable to climb those stairs to the second-floor balcony—the dark and damp corner where I swear I saw my great-great-grandmother Evarista's ghost. Decades later, I recognized the huge woman in the billowing white dress and the long, black hair that almost came down to the floor by a photograph my mother gave me—her appearance in El Colón during one of my childhood treks to a Saturday cartoon a branded memory I can never leave behind. I don't recall the Mexican cartoons or whether Benny, my cousin who always went to the movies with me, was there when the apparition scared the hell out of me and made me run down the balcony stairs to rejoin a crowd of kids jeering and laughing at the black-and-white images on the screen.

El Colón didn't open until 1919, though in 1910 the town had already boasted several silent movie houses on South El Paso Street, including El Alcazar, the Iris, El Hidalgo, the Eureka, the Paris, the Rex, and the Liberty. El Hidalgo became popular in June 1911 after it showed three reels of scenes from the first battle for Juárez, footage that has also disappeared, but was reportedly graphic in nature as the freewheeling camera crew filmed hundreds of dead and mutilated bodies lying in the dirt streets. The film was supposed to have also shown a rare glimpse of Dynamite Slim, an American mercenary who got his name from blowing up *federalista* trains across Chihuahua. He wore a Mormon-style beard and a broad hat during his adventures, but no one knows if he wore them in the film, and his presence in the film has never been verified. Like everything else I am searching for on South El Paso Street, Slim is gone.

Vendors from various stores stand on the sidewalk like carnival barkers, inviting pedestrians to come into their shops. Tables loaded with children's toys from Mexico, frying pans, irons, party favors, men's and women's socks, and other goods line the sidewalks. A poster on one storefront window announces bullfights in Juárez, the colorful poster of the mighty animal and the bullfighter printed in attractive black and red with a light brown background. I pause to study the poster and wish I could peel it off the window and take it with me for my collection. My interest in this kind of printing reminds me that some of the first El Pasoans to take advantage of the fighting in Juárez during the revolution were sidewalk postcard vendors. In the summer of 1911, after the first battle across the river, thousands of Mexicans and many foreign visitors fled Juárez and found refuge in El Paso. Many of them came up South El Paso Street on foot and passed these buildings, where, a few days after the battle, postcard sellers set up makeshift stands to sell black-and-white reproductions of dead bodies, troops in the streets, and devastated buildings. The *El Paso Times Herald* reported that "the market for Mexican war post-cards was as brisk these days as fur collars and fur boots." In August, the newspaper claimed the postcard vendors were gone as the revolution shifted to distant parts of Mexico, though there would be more than one battle of Juárez. In 1915, at the height of the war, the Mexican War Photo Postcard Company at 709 E. Fourth Street prospered near downtown. Walter Horne was the photographer, and he made a bundle by hawking bloody images to upper-class El Pasoans, who loved to collect the postcards. Many rich families lived in Sunset Heights, northwest of downtown, and its elevated bluffs above the Rio Grande were the ideal location to watch the fighting across the river.

Juan de Soto Martínez, a Mexican who worked for several of the elite families in Sunset Heights, wrote in his diary about a grand party on the rooftop of a mansion during the 1911 battle. He poured champagne into the glasses of several businessmen and their wives as they sat around a long table covered with a fine tablecloth. Their conversation and laughter were interrupted regularly by the echo of gunshots and exploding cannons across the river. Juan wrote about waiting on the party and about him and his bosses ducking stray bullets that zinged across the roof. He had to get up several times to keep pouring. During one quick and cautious filling of glasses, Juan noticed several dozen postcards someone had spread on the table. In between making toasts to the fine life in El Paso and pointing to troop movements across the river as more bullets flew by, party-goers shared the gruesome pictures and tried to identify familiar Juárez streets where they were taken. When someone recognized the main boulevard in front of La Virgen de Guadalupe Church in downtown Juárez, its lanes covered with dozens of dead bodies, a roar of congratulations and calls for more drinks rose above the distant gunfire. It was later reported that seventeen El Pasoans were killed by stray bullets during the battle. I wonder how many of them dropped handfuls of postcards as they fell from their observation posts.

Now I stare at the bullfight poster and can hear the breaking champagne glasses across the roofs of Sunset Heights. I have never seen any of the bloody postcards of the Juárez fight, though I found a series of cards showing the 1923 assassination of Pancho Villa in Parral, Mexico. They are housed in the Special Collections and Southwest Studies Center at the UTEP library. There are hundreds of photographs in history books about the Mexican Revolution, but the original postcards are as elusive as the Roma Hotel, Villa's mozo Joaquin, and my great-great-grandmother's ghost inside El Colón, their invisibility echoing louder in my head than the gunshots that Juan de Soto Martínez ducked. Whatever happened to the diary writer? Did many Mexican laborers keep written records of their struggles to feed themselves and their families by working across the river? Where is everybody I used to know in my old city? South El Paso Street reminds me of Juárez, not my hometown. The transformation is that complete. I don't ask the vendor inside the store for the bullfight poster, though I notice a rack of El Paso postcards near the counter, common shots of the Franklin Mountains and missions in the area not suitable for my own post-card collection back home in Minnesota. I do not own Mexican Revolution postcards. Rock-and-roll postcards, mostly of Bob Dylan and the Beatles, plus hundreds of cards from art galleries all over the country make up a good portion of my two thousand cards.

Glancing at my watch, I hurry back to my car parked at a meter a few blocks away because I don't want to get a ticket. As I walk briskly past storefronts I have never entered, thoughts about El Paso's lower crime rate return. There is one person left on my search list, and he must join my roll of the invisible. I pass the old site of the Roma Hotel and wonder if it was ever robbed by a daring hold-up man nicknamed Cara de Caballo (Horse Face), a bandit who terrorized South El Paso Street in 1920. During his numerous robberies, he wore a mask resembling the face of a horse. When he was finally arrested in 1921, he was identified only as "Murillo from Juárez," making his brief appearances on South El Paso like my great-great-grandmother and Villa's pigeons, whose flapping wings from his second-floor window are a sudden departure into the present as today's city birds suddenly rise from the concrete and are the last thing I hear as I walk past the bus stop with the lonely Aztec calendar and find a parking ticket on the window of my car.

I enter the Maze after reading about its grand opening and am quickly engulfed in claustrophobia, though the smarter part of me sees I could eas-ily break through the ten-foot-tall, neatly manicured cornstalks and run to my car. I barely make it around two corners, then turn around and get out of there. It is a seventeen-acre cornfield maze that opened a few days ago in La Union, New Mexico. It has a different design each year, and this fall the ninetieth-anniversary logo of UTEP and Paydirt Pete, the UTEP sports mascot, are designed into the field. In existence for five years, the Maze lured thirty thousand visitors in 2004 and took most calm people at least half an hour to get through it. I hear from friends that it is especially chal-lenging at night in the light of glow sticks, a time when I do not plan to try the Maze again. I stand there in the middle of the day and wonder why so many kids enter and disappear as if the odd structure of corn is as natural as the desert surrounding it.

Religious doubt and pondering appear several years after Julia, my grand-mother, passed away. This puzzlement over faith is also a sign for letting go of several of the last stories she told me before she died in 2000, at the age of ninety-six. If her presence is repeated throughout several of my journeys I have collected here, it is because these stories are vital in breaking with the past and seeing the old town replaced by the dwellings of a new century. Yet it always comes down to traditional, border faith—that connection with the desert ground where I believe true worship begins. It does not begin in the stone towers of contradiction. My grandmother gave me the following tale as an example of this source of faith that has to be tapped, in some manner, in the midst of upcoming sealed borders:

Julia told her grandson Alfredo his belly button was a gift, but did not say where the gift came from. One night, she put him to bed and Alfredo raised his T-shirt to stare at his belly button.

"Why is it a gift, Grandma?" he asked. "Who gave it to me?"

The old woman smiled at Alfredo. "The earth gave you your *ombligo*."

Alfredo did not understand. "The earth?"

His grandmother tucked him in and ran her hand over his forehead. "When your mother had you, I took a handful of mud from our garden and rubbed it on her belly."

"You did?" Alfredo's eyes widened. "Yuck! Didn't that make her dirty?"

His grandmother laughed. "No, Alfredo. Your mother needed her mother to help her bring you to us." She sat on the edge of the bed, made sure her grandson was covered by the blanket, and told him about the mud that helped his birth. She said that when the rains came, families were ready to bring their sons and daughters into the world. The mothers could not give birth until their mothers covered them with soft mud from the gardens surrounding their houses. It was the only way to assure a safe birth, even if the mud washed off before delivery. Mothers and daughters had been doing this for generations. Alfredo's mother, Lencha, followed her mother into their garden hours before Alfredo's birth. Julia and her daughter knew it was time by the way the sun baked the mud left by the rainstorm that morning. The women removed their shoes and stepped into a puddle. They held hands and splashed their feet. Mud flew up and covered them. Julia stepped out of the puddle, reached down with both hands, and grabbed the dripping mud. Lencha leaned back to let her mother rub her stomach with the dark, sticky earth.

"The earth is clean, Lencha," Julia said.

Lencha stood there with her round belly, then bowed down to grab more mud. Both women were silent as the daughter applied mud to her mother. Julia's thin stomach was completely covered with a shiny layer.

"The earth is clean, Mama," Lencha whispered.

Julia nodded and embraced her daughter. Now she described this moment to Alfredo, who listened quietly.

"But why is the earth clean when there is so much dirt?" he asked.

Julia laughed. "Yes, Alfredo, there is a lot of dirt, but it is on the ground to show us how many boys have been born."

Alfredo yawned and thought about these things. "But how did I get my belly button? Did it come from the dirt?"

Julia shook her head. "No, Alfredo. Your ombligo is a sign the earth let go of you as a gift to your mother." Julia continued, "When the mud covered your mother's stomach, it released its spirit into her body. When a baby is born, the ombligo is the arm of the earth letting go. The hands I used to cover your mother with mud and the hands of the earth held each other through your belly button."

Alfredo's eyes lit up. "Like shaking hands!" he exclaimed.

Julia smiled and loved the boy more. "Yes, like shaking hands. Your ombligo is the spot where your mother shook hands with the earth. When you are born, the handshake is over, and your belly button is left as a sign that your mother and the earth agreed to bring you to us."

Alfredo studied his ombligo, then pulled the blanket up to his chin. "Goodnight, Grandma," he said.

"Goodnight, Alfredo," Julia whispered. She leaned over him and kissed him on the forehead.

As she started to leave, Alfredo asked, "Grandma?" She paused in the doorway. "Did your mother shake hands with the earth when you were born, too?"

Julia nodded, "Yes, she did that a long time ago."

"So the earth is older than you?" Alfredo asked in wonder.

His grandmother laughed. "Yes, the earth is older than your grandmother. Goodnight, Alfredo." The boy sighed deeply as she closed the door.

From *Tarahumara of the Sierra Madre* by John G. Kennedy: "The god Onuruame is 'The One Who Is Our Father' or also known as Tata Riosi, who assimilated with the Christian god brought by the conquering Spanish." I stare at that passage in a book about a tribe of native people from northern Mexico I know nothing about, though my grandmother used to mention the Tarahumaras. What catches my eye is the word *Tata* because it is what I used to call my father before the age of five, when I finally learned English. Many infants who speak Spanish call their fathers "Tata." I will say little about my father's family here because it is a different story, though I see the connection between Julia's birth story and these Tarahumara deities.

Another passage lists Diablo or Rere Bateame, the "one who lives below and is often disguised as a serpent or a fox." This Diablo lives "under the river." The last Tarahumara deity I make note of is Oweruame, the shaman or "great curer," whose most important power is his ability to see.

The word *ancestor* is invisible and brings back the past as it makes us wonder about the future and how we select the parts of the present we shall forget. The word *ancestor* is a mystery and the clearest light of all. When we dig up old photographs of our grandparents, they look into the camera because tomorrow never goes away—yellowing images of those who stare at us from a time we can never know. The word *ancestor* is a sentimental history of family upheaval and reunion, stories passed on and changed to make us wonder what it must have been like to live back then. The word *ancestor* is the darkness of documents, a silent record of who was born and lived, and when they died. It is the sound of unanswerable questions—Who was my great-great-grandfather? What happened to my great-great-great-grandmother? At what point does knowledge of previous generations fade into the past, never to be retrieved? Did our ancestors know who came before them? How far back could they trace the origins of the family? What did each of them do to survive and feed their children? The word *ancestor* is carried in the heart like an invisible thread to people we shall never meet, the sound of their conversations inside tiny adobe houses lost somewhere in the challenge of imagining and re-creating those times. It is a word for our roots, yet it stands for what we don't realize about ourselves because the dialog between a grandfather and son is a private lesson. The embrace between grandmother and mother was a farewell that changed the source of our origins because the two people who became our parents met in a different town and year.

The idea of ancestry weaves itself across borders that are fenced, then torn open, migrations beyond love and hate becoming journeys where a few family members die as others cross into new territory. The perception of what came before is rewritten to warn us that we are heading in the wrong direction—the river and mountains of family characteristics lie over there. Their course and peak of shadows trace a tale where an uncle disappears, an aunt goes crazy, and mercenaries hired by a landowner kill a great-grandfather. No one survives to get it right, the details of a certain evening along the river added to a different episode where a grandmother got married, her father threatening the groom for coming from the wrong village, the fires in the town celebrating the departure of another clan. Few are told the truth as the first baby boy is born and the next two sons are a sign that daughters will be hard to find. When half the family leaves for the North, they make sure the quiet uncle stays behind. He is not the one who disappeared, but the one who has secrets and learned the tricks of many trades from the local *curandero*—a fact no ancestor wants to admit or allow to be traced to his or her home. The moment of the ancestor arrives when this quiet uncle weaves magic with words and little scraps of paper he hides in his bedroll. When the sole photograph of this man is found in the antique trunk, no one can say what happened to him, the hat he wears bristling with flowers and twisted leaves, his hands holding a strange object, perhaps the family heirloom everyone has been whispering about for one hundred years.

El Calvario's priest for decades was Padre Pacheco. When I walked by the old stone church as a six-year-old, I didn't know that the old priest had played a role in the lives of my mother's family for decades. In 1929, as a young priest in Benson, Arizona, Padre Pacheco had baptized my mother. Twenty-one years later, after everyone in the family moved to El Paso, the padre would marry my parents in El Calvario, where I was later to be baptized. The tall steeple of the church is an image I have carried with me since I was a child, and passing it daily after getting off the bus from school helped to implant that memory in my mind. I sometimes believe that one of my earliest memories is my baptism. I can make out a crowd of guests in the church and feel my parents holding me before Padre Pacheco as he performs the ritual of blessing me with the holy water.

I didn't know about the old Arizona friendship between my grandparents and the priest. As the wife of a railroad crew foreman who was gone a great deal of the time, my grandmother had plenty of time to make a potent home brew from yeast during the Prohibition years of the 1930s. She got a reputation among the railroad workers in Benson for making some of the best beer in the desert. She poured it into ceramic jugs that were distributed among the men. My mother told me how Bonifacio, my grandfather, got Padre Pacheco drunk on the home juice one Saturday night. The priest was so drunk that he missed Sunday service the next morning, and there was a local scandal over it. It didn't help that Padre Pacheco had a mistress in town and that the woman herself had a fine reputation as a drinker.

After my grandfather died young in 1941 and my mother's family moved to El Paso, connection with Padre Pacheco was lost for a few years.

One day someone summoned a priest for a very ill woman who lived next door to my great-grandmother's house, where Julia, my grandmother, was living in the early years of relocating to El Paso. When a priest showed up to perform the last rights, Julia recognized the priest from Arizona. The friendship continued until Padre Pacheco died in the mid-1960s, several years after El Calvario was torn down.

One individual whose actions have probably never gotten into most history books, though they have a great deal to do with how Mexican and Texan history developed, is Juan Mena. As another person on my list of the invisible, Mena could have taught me about breaking old bonds. He was born in Santa Rosalio, near Monterey, Mexico, in 1817 and entered Benito Juárez's army at the age of twelve. He fought for the first great Mexican leader of the modern era and had a long career in the army. Mena was the soldier who led the firing squad that executed Emperor Maximilian, the French dictator who ruled over Mexico in the mid–nineteenth century. On June 19, 1867, Mena fired the mercy shot into Maximilian after a volley of shots ended French rule in North America and the rebellious Mexicans declared their independence. After the revolt, Mena moved to San Antonio, Texas, where he worked in a butcher shop for many years. Then he moved to El Paso and resided there for seventeen years. He spent his final years in Alamogordo, New Mexico, and lived to be 109 years old. He could be seen walking the streets of Alamogordo in his final years, finally dying there in 1926. Juan Mena is not famous like Pancho Villa or Maximilian, but the fact that he left the dramatic stage of political events around Mexico City and went north says a great deal, though I don't know anything about his life in El Paso. He may have continued his trade as a butcher in town, though he would have died before meeting one of my uncles, Jesús Silva, who was one of the best butchers in El Paso in the 1950s and early 1960s. Tío Chutis, as my mother called him, was famous for a great chorizo recipe that was a hit in butcher shops all over South El Paso. He made the spicy Mexican sausage himself, refusing to give my mother his secret recipe for it each time she asked. As a small boy, I remember Tío Chutis and the way he joked with my mother and me when he came to visit. He is not on my list of the invisible because I see him pulling up in his old Ford, getting out, tossing jokes at my mother even before he gets to the front door with a package of chorizo under his arm. In contrast, I try to imagine Juan Mena and wonder how he felt about putting the final bullet into Maximilian. I would love to ask him what brought him to El Paso. One of my sisters is married to a Mena, my brother-in law coming from one of the better-known family lines in the area. Could Juan Mena, executioner of an emperor, be related?

My friend Peter and I have no choice but to bring humor to our Thanksgiving rendezvous in El Paso. We always get heavy about growing up in the place. Visiting his mother's grave and driving around Northeast El Paso make for a long day of nostalgia for what is gone. So I can't help myself and start right in from the back seat of his car as he drives and his daughter sits in the front.

"Why hasn't Osama Bin Laden crossed into the United States through Juárez?" I ask.

They shrug.

"Because Arabs can't swim," I say. The three of us shake our heads at the racist joke, the entry of such sick stuff common in our life-long friendship, though there are no "Jews versus Mexicans" jokes this time.

"Why did Osama Bin Laden stay in Juárez and open a taco stand?" I ask.

No comment.

"Because he had to do something with his dead camel," I answer.

"What is Osama Bin Laden's favorite food?" I keep trying and have to provide the answer. "Beans because in the caves of Bora Bora, they are known as weapons of mass destruction."

I give up after this last one: "How can you tell if Osama Bin Laden has been in your refrigerator?"

I thought one of them would have the answer, but no, so I say, "By the beard in the ice cream."

From *Origins of New Mexico Families: A Genealogy of the Spanish Colonial Period* by Fray Angélico Chávez: "Domingo Gonzalez. 'El Gallego' (The Galician). Native of the Spanish province of Galicia and 40 years of age in 1664. He was living in Santa Fe with his wife Francisca Marten. Three years later, he was dead. He died 16 years before the Pueblo Indian Revolt against the Spanish colonies in New Mexico."

This is the earliest listing of a Gonzalez in New Mexico I have found in my genealogical searches. I have no idea if he is related to my father's family, though my uncle Jose has told me that the Gonzalez family had several large cattle ranches in northern New Mexico before they made their way down to the El Paso area. But if Domingo was one of the first, if not the first, Gonzalez to settle the area, the line could have started with him. He died young, and the genealogical record doesn't say why. I search other names of the same period and discover a number of entries that refer to how many men in Santa Fe got rich at the expense of the natives and which ones refused to leave Santa Fe during the 1680 revolt and wound up killed by the Pueblos. I mention this fact knowing that Domingo was long dead by that time, but it reminds me of the Gonzalez tradition in a number of ways.

At the same dinner with my sisters where the topic of Mel Gibson's *The Passion of the Christ* came up, I asked if any of them had recently visited our grandmother Julia's grave, which is in a new cemetery on the eastern edges of El Paso, a good twenty-five miles from my mother's house. One of my sisters says she was out there a few months ago, but the other two have not taken flowers in a long time. I ask without reminding everyone that I have not been to her grave since attending her funeral five years earlier. I have not gone to visit because, for me, her passing and the deaths of three other relatives in El Paso around the same time took place from afar. I live in Minnesota, so family illness, the aging process, and older generations disappearing from our lives have not affected me the way they have impacted my family in El Paso. As part of breaking with the past, I have placed the recent deaths of people who were close to me at a distance, these tragedies happening without me. My absence has turned inevitable events into an extinction that places sadness at arm's length and adds another dimension to the historical extinction I find on South El Paso Street because the people I knew most of my life have joined the invisibility of the past. I will repeat what I said earlier—my hometown is gone, along with the dead. Its absence is part of my own aging and my lifelong artistic struggle with capturing the past in my writing. *Extinction* is the appropriate word because the historical characters I search for on South El Paso wait somewhere for my ancestors to join them in the history books of the heart and mind. I have not been able to get myself to make the long drive to the other end of town and place flowers on the grave of Julia Canales, not even a stone to mark a weeping or a final letting go. This feeling moves beyond grief or some naive, romantic pining for the good old days because on the U.S.–Mexican border, this embrace of history, both public and private, has been a traditional element in the way El Paso and Juárez have conducted their relationship with one another. On the border, you must speak to the dead, the historically famous, and the anonymous faces that populate old hotels and movie houses. You must do so in order to find a better way to live in the present, to deal with a vast region that feeds off the past as it tries to prosper in the twenty-first century. As I let go of the recent dead, I wonder how the coming of the National Guard will affect the dynamics of old and new in a place that has always depended on what once was in order to move forward, day by day.

If I keep writing about the same things, over and over, what have I failed to say? What am I unable to approach about El Paso? What am I unable to escape? These memories are not about the past, but about the present moment of recognizing my hometown without trying to identify what has changed it on a massive scale. Its history has already been told, and I need to live within that record, both public and private. Author Paul Auster writes in *The Invention of Solitude*, his book about memory and family, "Memory, then, is not so much about the past contained within us, but as proof of our life in the present. If a man is to be truly present among his surroundings, he must be thinking not of himself, but of what he sees. He must forget himself, in order to be there. And, from that forgetfulness arises the power of memory. It is a way of living one's life, so that nothing is ever lost." So, perhaps, this invisibility of things around me is part of the process of forgetting in order never to leave behind any of my ancestors, early experiences, or my original El Paso.

I can miss my grandmother or my tío Boni, ponder what happened to Joaquin, Villa's mozo, or attempt to get near the glass doorways of El Colón to sense the spirit of a great-great-grandmother I never knew, but their invisible character, clothing, and voices will never close the distance between 1911 and 2006. My hometown is gone, and I wander through a different El Paso, loving it as I have never loved it before and wishing the ghosts of history could reenact every lost detail I need for my writing. All they do is stand in absent balconies, closed alleys, and torn-down doorways and stare at me. The past is on South El Paso Street and among the green lawns of the new cemetery where my grandmother lies. I can't go there because every invisible heart already walks with me toward the future.

Renaming the Earth

Whatever evaluation we finally make of a stretch of land, however, no matter how profound or accurate, we will find it inadequate. To intend to preserve some of the mystery within it as a kind of wisdom to be experienced, not questioned. And, to be alert for its openings, for that moment when something sacred reveals itself within the mundane, and you know the land knows you are there.

—Barry Lopez, *Arctic Dreams*

The great bend of the Rio Grande at Hatch, New Mexico, opens for me each time I stand on the south bank and gaze across the water. When I step to the edge of the desert, the men who walked there centuries ago rise out of the ground, and they are afraid. When I step to the edge of their nightmares, they drop their maps and run into the canyons, their robes on fire. When I step to the edge of my world, I cannot read the pictures on the tablets, but take a guess as to what the signs on the rocks mean, where the storm will hit, and how I will step into the dusty dimension of an earth that no longer needs me—the dust of a thousand years reshaping the fault in my story. When I step to the edge of a lie, I look down at my hands and can't believe what I hold, its weight cutting into the threaded passage between truth and the way everything has been on the part of the earth where I grew up. When I step to the edge of the campfire, it is the strangest thing I have ever done because there is no one there, the last smoke drifting beyond the site, the heat in the arm of the Rio Grande demanding I come this far to pray that the old cottonwoods finally fall into the water, the splash to be heard one century later when those men who survived get up again, their dreams never reaching the western sea.

Consejos Canyon lies somewhere on the eastern edges of the Gila Wilderness, near the ghost town of Cloride, New Mexico. It is not on a map and can never be traced or plotted on a tourist guide; I entered it in my twenty-sixth year, maybe a year after first visiting the hacienda near Chamberino. The arches over the canyon were natural and rare in this part of New Mexico, their fine layers of sandstone crusting into shapes I thought were familiar. As I entered a shaded hollow of twisted cottonwoods, I realized the crumbling walls of the canyon had to be read in a different manner. Though I had just started my walk, I paused and drank from my canteen.

This is the last detail I can recall from that hike. Ponderosa pines, ocotillo, and mesquite crowd my memory, and the endless rocks leading to a distant peak I never reached weave colors across the things I want to remember about the hike into Consejos, steps I had to take to rename the earth under my feet. I want to recall that hike because in my early twenties I did not find new words for the earth. As a young man, I made the mistake of not renaming familiar territory in order to give it new life that would keep me going as a son of the desert and as a writer. Though I had not explored Consejos before, it was familiar because I had entered many other canyons, each one unique in its shadows, every one the same in the way they swallowed a landscape that had not released me when I was so young.

It took hours to get where I was going, and it took hours to climb out of the earth. I found something up there, but cannot describe it now. If I added to my fossil collection that day, I took something away. If I paused at the deepest turn in the canyon, I thought I saw markings high up on the walls. Whatever I noticed, I lost because I did not have a name for it. If I had, it would have replaced a familiar older name—the title required to immerse oneself in a desert that has waited five hundred years to be renamed.

> And suddenly, hazy in the light, the ancient tower, raised between yesterday and tomorrow. I remember the stairway, the worn steps, the nausea and vertigo.
> —Octavio Paz, *Eagle or Sun?*

These tracks are for believers, climbers who paused here and looked down, those arms of ocotillo twisting their thorns around their sweating necks, taking them to the place I have heard about, but have never reached because I fell before getting there. The line of river below does not wait, its blue vein taking me where others have passed without opening their eyes, black rocks smoothing my hands with an order for clouds, rain, even the smoke from an ancient site I know nothing about. These sticks are for makers, planners, men who hid in the mountains and belonged to secret societies of dirt and streaked faces—tongues lashing in and out, extracting beads from the plant, biting the oil from the root before blessing the throat by swallowing what is alive and waiting to be taken into ground space that existed long ago, before any of this took place. These feet are for the earth wall, disappearing into crevices of gold and the mistaken cut in the cliff that shows me where the signature goes, where it snows in heat and doubt, where I can scratch the word and get away with it because everything has flown and the only flat surface up here is reserved for hiding the true opening, an entrance into the earth I have heard about, but have not been able to open in fifty-six years of my life.

At the Bear Paws–White Rock Shelter Excavation site, Franklin Mountains, El Paso.

    To touch the iron face, he smoothes the rock. To kiss the rock, he waits for the bear, ancient fury leaving white prints on the walls, pushing crooked arrows into what never was, drawing bear paws in circles, blood first, paint second, claiming the cave for learning and dreaming, digging and dying. To trace the iron face, he eats nothing. To wet the stones, he hears the bear, knows its song will move to the other side of the mountain, the council where he is given a place among the dancers who lost the moon the last time they stormed the bear. To change the iron face, he drinks water. To exchange the walls, he sees the bear, its dark hips destroying the wind of its second guessing, the way the rocks come down to cover the sign painted before he faces the animal and his hands turn white in the dawn of good fires, the cave swallowing what happens next.

Look at the dead mimosa tree, how your hands stayed there. Be proud of the pollen that hid in your hair when it was time to flee and not be followed. There is a forgotten tune, and it is ancient, hidden inside the vein no one traces until their death. There is a shadow, and it is called ancient home—structures erased from their seed to grow elsewhere, vultured strings searching for a frame that stands atop history and renames the ground, marking the heart with lipstick, necklaces of grief—the perfect amulet swallowed by the frantic lover who left you under the tree. Look at the dead mimosa limbs. Blink at the return of the swaying sky, doubt colored by winter's knee, the gray asking if you are there, wondering how those branches reach places you can't see. It is what binds you. How long have you known this when you go there alone? When you return, make a list of what you found—escarpments moving the horizon, great timbers painting the sky as the mimosa stays alive.

Frontera Norte Sur, April 23, 2002:

> In an attempt to mitigate odors coming from a wastewater treatment facility in Méxicali's Zaragoza neighborhood, Méxicali's Dirección de Ecología (Office of Ecology) has begun planting 6,000 trees on the banks of a waste treatment pond. Another 9,000 trees will be planted in future phases of the project. According to Alejandra León Gasté-lum, head of the Dirección de Ecología, the trees are all from species that absorb odors and should reduce odors around the treatment plant by 60 percent. Her office is also in the midst of testing some chemical products to see if they could help mitigate the problem.

I plant a tree in the mountains and tell no one where I dug the hole and left the young thing. I have no idea if it will grow and can't explain why I went to a nursery in El Paso and bought a young tree for almost one hundred dollars, then drove into the mountains with it. I do not reveal what kind of tree it is because to give away its name would mean I am taking language beyond itself—forcing an idea of what the tree is and how it might survive in the wilderness. I plant a tree in secret and wonder if it has the ability to absorb odors, though the pure scents of a mountain top do not need to be swallowed by well-meaning intentions or the power of six thousand trees.

I plant one tree and go away, climb down the steep trail to get as far as I can from my outdoor game because I have fulfilled a secret need to do this after realizing I have gone too far into the Franklin Mountains without leaving anything behind. This has gone on for years, and I know I am not supposed to leave a trace up there, the eroding peaks overlooking El Paso as if their vast tables have waited for fresh unveilings and new discoveries—not many places left to excavate without intruding on fresh housing developments sneaking up the mountains.

I plant one tree and do not repeat the language I have learned in my hundreds of walks through the desert. I cannot repeat those words because to recite them would give me fresh ideas about how to get out, how to mark the stone path below me with something I can accurately describe without sounding lame. I make sure the new tree is in the right spot, surrounded by vegetation and other growth I am not supposed to touch. Yet I touch them and come down from the mountain with muddy hands.

By summer the air will leave an after-word, and the absence will unknot the grass, open it to waters that carry the moon away. Why are you disappointed? By the hand that feeds the soil and the shadows that close eyelids, you will have to answer. In the dawn of the flyway, in the rotting path to the adobe wall, the child turns away from the truth. Where does downstream begin, tracing the contour of the cottonwood until it no longer serves your wish? In the search for the desert wind, a fading signature in the fields. Beside the red mountain of faith, the rains that punish the cemeteries. By the accomplished hand of the mud and the stroke of the ancient brush, feet move closer to the painted boulder. To live without reading the earth is to breathe in the remnants of the moon, and all of this will be repeated. If to leave your burning house says you never looked at the night sky, you stepped too close to the tree that never broke in the heat. Why do you keep digging? When you stand in the sweat of leaving, you are quiet. When the burden pollinates the vines, your hands are suddenly covered in the tempting green.

Bitter and sweet, our blackberry bush gives us its first two clusters of berries, dark purple beads my wife pops in her mouth. She loves the taste, says it is one of the best things she has ever eaten. Days later it is my turn, but my bunch is too bitter, juicy and smart as I swallow what I didn't have and never should have plucked with such desire. I want the blackberry bush to give me more as it grows larger, so it can cover the space between joy and the curious tongue, spread across the brown mounds of a hidden fruit and fill its shadow with thorns bleeding purple like my tongue. The first taste of those berries is an act of sharing a judgment and its liquid, a pinch of wine my wife and I have cherished between us, waiting for thorns of the blackberry bush to show us our dusty glasses are full and starting to tremble.

Not for the sake of the hands inside the plant, wishing they were cut off by a harmless root that wraps itself around the giving of those hands, petals mistaken for the course of the sun, the awful growth of humus, parchment, and the cut thorn inside the root that can never be seen. Not for the beauty of a meaningless word that thought it could reinvent love as a window beside the roar of the man who knew how to adopt silence whenever he broke eggs open on the stone oven, cooked them as the hungry king that always knew how to guess which wing brought him food, which sound brought him wisdom, which monkey in the trees brought him a way out of the castle.

Not for the many friends who have gathered to grow old and establish themselves as elderly men who quit carving odd lines into the walls of their tiny rooms, sayings the spider and the cockroach escaped with the slap of the hand and wandered across those walls. Not for the gift of the fire ants crawling up the legs of the man mowing the lawn, dozens of them biting him as if the giant earth didn't belong, climbing up his legs to redesign them as a country they can possess with millions of eggs lying under the ground the mower can't reach. Not for the song found in an old vinyl record scratched beyond the years of working the guitar that wouldn't come back, a pop or two bouncing from speaker to speaker as if the unplugged diamonds of the heart were coming back on stage for an encore.

Not for the knot in the tree my father never cut down, the one cottonwood still standing by the house where I was born, the only tree never swept away in the flood, until I had to grip it with both hands, tear it out of the ground, embed it in my heart. Not for the mud traveling where I found red-and-white worms when I was digging a hole to plant a new blackberry bush I bought when the sun owed me something. The worms jumped and twisted in the mud, flashed into the black face of the morning mud and disappeared until I dug them up, glistening strings reshaping themselves into thoughts I quit having long ago—thick worms scattering before the shovel of the digger who knows how to avoid a place he can't reach. Not for the way I came out of my mother with a large head and no neck. Not for the way I grew short and fat and had to learn sounds from the fruit of silence—repeating what scares me when I wake to find nothing there.

I rename the earth to give myself time, find useful words and phrases for revived categories of history—those abstract forces that have guided me across the Chihuahua Desert my entire life. I rename the earth to get to know it again, the newly dug radioactive site near Carlsbad and the NAFTA highway between the United States and Mexico erasing old fires, worn labels, and the alphabet that is stamped on each thing we do before we begin to understand we have had the power to replace given names all along. I rename the ground to be able to step on it again, my worn sneakers covered in dry mud because they are the only ones I can wear to get from one rock to another, one path to one arroyo without slipping down and having to rename my wounds—those cuts and bruises I loved to write about when I was a boy, burying my physical treks in the desert inside tiny notebooks that could not see the light of day or be read by anyone except the person renaming everything around him.

I rename everything because the new century demands it, the blood and terror of an angry world moving across the Rio Grande almost in the same manner it moves across the Twin Towers and the streets of Baghdad. This is not an exaggeration because to rename things means to recognize how the invisible border between my home and Mexico is going to explode as more people come across and more people try to stop them. I rename their flight across the electrified desert to play the game.

I was tired of the disabling light, couldn't look at the pictures of the mummies in the burial chambers any longer because one of the well-preserved bodies looked like someone I knew long ago. No one warned me that the translators of the accompanying text were actually re-creating hallucinations that arose from the mummies of a forgotten civilization. Theories over their culture were debated until they disappeared like invisible ink from tablets whose symbols knew exactly where to go.

Once, when I toured the mission at San Elizario, I saw an old man watching me from a dim corner of the sanctuary, his long white hair hanging down his eyes, a mop in his hands, and a green-and-red paper butterfly tied to some of his braids. I stood up from genuflecting and making the sign of the cross, and he was gone, the sounds of shuffling feet behind the altar turning to votive candles lit suddenly by hidden hands. As I walked out into the blinding sunlight, I knew I could pray without my eyes, yielding to the love of words as quickly as a starfish embedded in a desert fossil, its motions remembered as I turned to look for the old man one more time. Perhaps he couldn't speak, only hurtle himself into a ball like the Belmez faces, those profiles on a cottage floor in Spain that come and go, reappearing even after the concrete is replaced, eyes translated into what I am trying to see.

When I saw the lizard asleep in the weeds, I was alone and startled it. It disappeared before I could capture it and hold it under a magnifying glass, searching for its third eye. If the reptile was to secrete anything onto my hand, I could be blinded, but I also know that secretion is another century of darkness, a third ground where the tiny claws of nervousness scratch messages on my palm to rival those patterns cut into the stones around the mummies in the pictures.

I have always loved this disabling mirror of history and time, the one that shoots a burning light into the eyes of those who want to dig up the past, write about it, or hold its remains in their hands. My teachers have shown me how to look when I cared to rival the sun and its light, learning which of my eyes to open first, when to blink, when simply to stare. How often this seeing leads to difficulty, the numerous mummies buried in desert ground under my feet disintegrating without my being aware of them because I have searched too often with closed eyes.

I drive through Colorado and New Mexico and am amazed at the power and beauty of landscapes I can only appreciate from a distance. The Rocky Mountains, the Sangre de Cristos, the Organ Mountains, and the Rio Grande. The list is endless, and the sights are overpowering. As a native of the Southwest, I grew up in the midst of vast landscapes, and they helped to make me a writer. I have written about this before, but on this recent journey I realized that most of us love and admire landscape from a distance. Driving down Interstate 25 from Denver to Albuquerque to El Paso, I saw countless forests, mountain ranges, river valleys, and wild animals. Yet I admired them from far away. I was driving for hundreds of miles and could look off to distant peaks and rivers, but when I actually drove to some of these places and got out to smell the air, the image and shape of the land in the distance was gone. There was nothing there, and then, suddenly, there it was because perception came into play and kept me going and looking to see distance as vision and vision as unapproachable distance. I was there and not there.

We admire images of snowy peaks, red canyons, and rushing rivers from many miles away. When we are actually there, on the riverbank or in the middle of a trail to the top of Pike's Peak, we can't see what we admired from so far way because we are on top of it. Common sense, yet the power of the distant image is gone, and the terrain or body of water is upon us, changing our vision and perceptions, erasing the panorama that drew us there in the first place. We can enjoy the hike and the water or watch mountain blue jays jump from tree to tree, but it is not the same thing as being twenty miles from the peak or the canyon and observing them from there. At that remote point, our vision and emotional responses are different than when we are standing on the actual spot.

Once, when I was driving toward the Grand Canyon years ago, the majestic chasms in the earth frightened me. My family and I were still about thirty miles from the actual park and South Rim, but the openings in the earth confused our senses, left us in awe, and drew us magnetically to our final destination. Once we saw the actual canyon and spent time on the rim in the midst of too many tourists, the magic had already worn off. Even standing on the edge of incredible drop-offs did not affect me the same as getting there. The magnetism was gone. My body and its senses were now part of the landscape and no longer trying to get there, in the middle of readjusting my heart rate, my vision, and my sense of balance as I had to while driving there. Distant landscapes change our feelings toward the earth and draw us in. Once we are in the heart of that landscape, though, everything has changed. Again, standing on the edge of the Grand Canyon or reaching the top of Aguirre Springs in the Organ Mountains of New Mexico is not the same experience as getting there.

Image.

Distance.

Color.

Height.

Deepness.

They work together to get us there, and we know that landscape way over there will not be there when we get to it. It is gone, and the earth is in our face, surrounding us with a magnetism that drew us to it, but that is now transformed into a living, breathing environment that has taken us into itself. The landscape has vanished from our eyes and our bodies, even from the two feet that kept us balanced as we climbed to reach it. Yes, we enjoy walking along the Rio Grande, but the great river is more appealing from far away—its long ribbon of muddy light meandering through the desert as it generates daydreams and memories of a desert past.

Each time I make it over the curve on Interstate 25 south of Hatch, New Mexico, I spot the ribbon of blue light in the Mesilla Valley below. The river extends as far as I can see, and as I drive, it keeps getting farther from me, as if I can never reach a special place along its banks I have been trying to get to my whole life. Distance and evasiveness. Distance and intense beauty. Remoteness erased when we are close enough to touch the actual that created such vistas. When I cross a highway bridge over the Rio Grande, it is the water of home and not a remote landscape. There is a great difference between the two because the aura of the river's course attracts me to it, yet its water makes every possible idea of a distant river come true as I draw near it.

Taking my car slowly over the two-lane road into the Saguaro National Forest west of Tucson sets me before the incredible sight of thousands of bright green saguaros sticking up from the black and red rock canyons. This strange, almost primeval forest extends for miles. I take a chance and stop the car on the narrow road. I get out and gaze across the valley and know I have never seen anything like it—mile after mile of green sticks that disappear into the horizon. They look like thousands of army troops marching across the desert in vast, unorganized groups. I don't know how else to describe them. I get in my car and arrive at the park museum. Enormous saguaros thick as husky men stand all around me. Where is the army of green towers I came upon ten miles back? Here I am standing next to a twenty-foot-tall cactus, its twisted arms weaving the air above my head. Did I get to the place where I was going? Am I at the exact spot on earth that delivers the mystery and the detailed intricacies of a saguaro skin, its exterior form pockmarked with holes and cuts, its many limbs rotting on the ground?

The distance of landscape is made to draw us in, so we can say we have arrived in nature, and the natural world is all around us. Once we are there, the captivating light, colors, and designs of the leeways have done their job. They have taken the visual expanse of the world, placed it before us, and waited for us to arrive. I remind myself that I have been reaching for those distances as a writer and that those destinations have been right there the whole time. They have always been before me, miles away and just over the next bend in the dirt road. When I leave the center of a saguaro forest or turn away from the Rio Grande, I re-create the distance I am searching for and the sight of such power and grace—the tip of a snow peak on the Organ Mountains and the bend in the river will push and pull me as I measure what I have seen. When I leave and turn around to look, the landscape of tomorrow is there.

Giving the earth a new name is the act of threading the past with the present and hoping that it leads to a future where the vast desert can be what it has been, though signs of change are everywhere. It means taking what I have learned as a native of the Southwest and scrambling knowledge to find any overlooked secrets, both obvious and hidden facts coming alive in a time when geckos hang on the brick walls of my mother's house, tiny reptiles attracted to the porch light. My mother calls them "geckos," not "lizards." What happened to the many species of lizards I saw constantly when I was growing up? On top of that, the mighty scorpions have disappeared. My mother says she saw only two last summer and none so far this season. For years, scorpions invaded her house during the summer, and she perfected the art of killing them with her "scorpion stick." The scorpions are gone for good, and she has no idea why.

I use my memory to remember something from my past and lose some of the details when I write it down. I try to recall what happened, but can bring back only a few things—the pigeon I found limping down the garage driveway when I was seven years old; my cousin crying and running down the street when at the age of twelve I accidentally shot him in the ass with my BB gun after one of our hunting treks through the empty desert hills behind my house; the first time I saw a naked woman, the purple light in the room diminishing into a darkness that keeps me from recalling how old I was when she was there with me. I use that fading image to extract a detail I can hardly reconstruct because the shadows of time have arrived and are going to keep certain things secret to challenge me to dig toward things that may not want to be rediscovered.

I use memory to gaze upon a stream of water that runs slowly out of the ground to show me thought is actually the foundation for an intricate loss of color and design that displays few autobiographical meanderings—in other words, there is no salvation in looking down through the earth in my search for clarity from the past and a means to understand long-hidden emotions. This leaves the ground safe from excavation, and what lies buried must stay there because I can't remember the exact spot in the desert where at the age of fourteen I buried a large seashell. It was a brilliant pink-and-white bone swirl my cousin gave me when I visited her in California one summer. I kept it in my room for one year, then one day I had to give something back in the early years of being a teenager.

Thirty-six years later, how do I know this was my intention? I buried the seashell in dry sand deep inside an arroyo and forgot the location a few days later. How can I remember that that burial was completely erased from my mind so quickly? I never went back to try and find it, never thought much about the meaning of burying an artifact from the ocean in a dry desert much older than the sea. The memory makes me label the seashell an artifact when it is a fossil, its smooth, hard surface vanishing into a recollection that I had to get rid of it so I could put an end to childhood. This sounds melodramatic and too complicated for a teenager to think of doing, yet whatever made me bury the shell also made me erase much of those years, until the stream of water running brown through the dirt makes me look up at the cloudy sky, and I find myself gazing at a spot in the distance that brings the fractured past into clear light—the fact that we can remember only what arrives making us cling to these arrivals in disjointed use. The result is that I build from what happened long ago so I can set myself upon an island where reliving past moments becomes an isolated circle of incompletion—an eternal, mental dance of wanting to be back in the exact moment of experience that rises through the physical body and mind to devour our present, biological systems, created so we can't proceed with our days without having to mark memories of events, experiences, and encounters that changed the way we matured or stayed lost.

This devotion to hungering thoughts from ages ago feeds the memory, and we have difficulty remembering anything because we are living it, even if it already happened and we are standing staring at the sky from some distant point in the future. The white tent in the middle of a grassy field where I spotted an old woman emerging comes into focus and makes me want to run to her to see if she is my grandmother, dead five years, but this hypnosis is not about family, but about the way I encounter their ghosts, removing myself from the actual interaction of the past so I can run across the smooth hill, the white tent towering in front of me as a white bird springs for the trees. When I pause, out of breath, the tent folds into itself. I stand alone and listen to the river flowing rapidly on the other side of the trees. I have been here before and am disappointed that memoir signifies composing fractured dispositions that require the lone individual to wrestle with the consequences of remembering things. I stand by the Rio Grande, the river of my past, and do not know what its muddy waters carry after thirty years of living elsewhere. I can't quite see the opposite bank as I stumble through the tall reeds of yesterday. Those thirty years are not causing the current to overflow and are not getting me any closer to the high bank. I stand amidst tall, decaying cottonwoods (the most common tree found in my previous memoirs and how I have recorded what they have sheltered) and stare at the passing waters.

There is always an image behind my back of someone staring across a river, and I have not been able to rid myself of this recurring photo that has been imprinted in my brain since I left the desert thirty years ago. In trying to go back to something that already happened and can't be described in satisfying detail, I am immersed in the landscape of memory—the Rio Grande and its cottonwoods. How I got here I don't know because the limping pigeon I kept as a pet for a few weeks, before it disappeared, is the actual thing the memory is supposed to dispel—the idea of a boy wanting to heal a pigeon merely an avenue of the mind where helplessness, desire, and loss force a construct where I am the boy that held the pigeon, searching for a low cooing the bird never gave, and I am still the boy that cried when it vanished from the garage one day. This placement of the heart outside of its actual beating may be one accomplishment that allows me to see how fragile an action it was to think I could save and keep a wild yet common creature from the streets of early childhood. And it keeps fluttering back to childhood.

Why do so many memoirs wrestle with childhood? Why is it so important to go back to those early years? Plus, I haven't even dealt with the fact that the word *memoir* means I am trying to write something down, composing a personal story from a past that is efficient in scrambling grammatical building blocks because the idea of memoir is actually about the challenge of construction and not about the past itself. The faulty pigeon is a memory I think about at least once a year, and perhaps this pigeon of loss gets more credit than it deserves because I can never completely analyze what that dumb bird did to me. Plus, no one cares when such tiny acts in the daily actions of a small boy come and go, though they are imprisoned in time and are available for some kind of useful rapture that demands I bounce between then and now, wishing the geometrical flesh of my brain could figure it out and maybe allow the imperfect pigeon finally to limp out of me for good.

So my cousin Benny runs home crying with his arms behind him. His hands grip his ass through his jeans, my shock at my BB rifle accidentally going off not keeping me from following him into our house where my mother is pleading with him to tell her what happened. In between sobbing and holding his ass, my cousin announces I have shot him on purpose. My uncle and his family were visiting on a Saturday, and I don't remember what his reaction was to my shooting his son. I don't recall being scolded or punished, though I did try to set the record straight by insisting the rifle went off unintentionally, which is true. I don't recall who believed me or what my cousin did in retaliation. We used to play together quite often, and if one of us did something to hurt the other, there was always some form of quick, youthful revenge. I can't recall the consequences and am surprised that all I can see is my crying cousin running ahead of me, trying to get to the house because his cousin shot him in the ass with a BB pellet that never penetrated his skinny butt, but ricocheted into the air of time and invisibility, until that tiny, hard ball whistles across the backyard as I hit the seventh or eight sparrow off the telephone wires, a true hunger searching for my next target.

In and out of my house, the roots vanish. Few of my wife's plants did not make it. Fast bees a man keeps as a desperate gift. When the water comes, it spreads the story I can't tell. This is the house and this is the garden. When the tiny salamanders spring out of the hibiscus, I take my time coming back from the drum in my mouth. My words are for the huge frog that leaps out of the tomato plant, and my excuse for watering the magnolia is too long. No one wakes me when the rains return. I dream of windows embedded in the skull of the boy. No one whispers that it is time to repeat the formula for the garden. No one demands honor should stick to the forehead when you get down and dig. I step in the garden and crush what won't grow, search for the earthworm I allowed to escape. Within this pattern of seeds, I wait for the eel burrowing on the other side of the earth as the myth I wanted when I measured the garden. Smells of the black soil grasp everything.

I see the small body lying in the ground, manure and mulch mixing to stiffen tiny arms the way the roses, blue maze, and hibiscus twist into a season of death each gardener expects, branching decay over the limit of blossoms where I duck the buzz of the huge, black bee. I dig in the soil to replant the magnolia, uncover several huge earthworms. They wriggle in the mud like miniature snakes, trying to burrow back into the dirt. I want to cut one apart, think of swallowing it instead. I lift it onto the shovel as its red skin gleams and holds its chamber back, keeps the mud from forming new worms to take over my digging. I wait for the earthworms to disappear, go down into the strength of roots that won't be known for decades. I bend down, stick my fingers in the ground until the earthworms vanish. I can feel something start to grow at last. Under the bricks, my words disappear as the great push I avoided for years.

As a poet of the desert, I emerged from prehistoric landscapes to stumble over the ancient remains of people who knew poetry in a way I will never know, their lyrical vision recorded by rough hands that were the first part of their bodies to disappear when they were buried under the earth. The madness of desert vision comes from having the desert sand erode the pictographs on the walls at Hueco Tanks and seeing them reappear on different rocks. The language of canyon dreams is a vocal silence—a learned alphabet that I had to chip off the fossils left from a sudden flash flood, the rushing water opening the arroyo to let me in. This silence is taught in isolation because the Chihuahua Desert weaves the insanity of known and unknown dreams through the growing lines of barbed wire and Border Patrol electric sensors.

To come out of the desert means the Sierra Madres and the Rio Grande compose my poems before I even know the hallucinations of a 110-degree day were the first dreams I recalled as a child. To have them reappear as a sand storm over the Sierras or as wavy lines in the dry Rio Grande riverbed says the poem is already written for me, transcribed onto the sandstone without asking anything of my hands. The madness of stolen history comes from not being the sole creator of this art, this language woven on the red rocks at Abo to keep the message whole—others came before me, others saw the rattlesnake coil and strike, others fried it over the campfire, and only one or two of the wanderers dared climb the cliff and carve the snake's answer onto a timeless canvas.

The way of seeing poems is the way the two masks, the three eyes, and the burning horse turn yellow on the cave walls. And they have instantly been renamed by my placing them here. Their transfer from ancient experience to the modern boy wandering the desert takes place when the child has been allowed to live below the peaks of the Franklin Mountains, his hidden drawings safely tucked away in a dark place in his room. The madness arrives when the poet leaves and carries the cave wall in his head without further use for those cartoons, their exploding figures shaped in prehistoric reds and yellows, some of them shining on cliff faces too high to reach, their distant markings barely noticeable to the curious eye.

These conclusions are nothing new, no fresh way to say the poems originate elsewhere, with the brown, bare feet carrying them onto the page. These realizations are faced when the poet accepts the madness of heat and the broken wall of the eroding adobe, reshaping invisible letters into the voice of desert silence rising through sore knuckles. Desert silence—the lunacy of time and the passing centuries of kivas, Chaco Canyon prosperity, disappearance—the armored European riding the burning horse over the ridge. Desert silence began with conquest and the first time the native people broke the cross into pieces. Desert sound—the poet stumbling upon the remains and offering the reconstructed puzzle to the world, this sound the quietest silence of his composing wrists.

Again, a conclusion based on the fact that the desert landscape cannot leave the blood and heart of the writer because it belongs to the invisible tribes that knew the desert better than he ever did. Why the madness of staring at the walls as if others will come up here and pay attention? Because the border of today is the electrified barbed wire of a hidden camera lens that tracks thousands of illegal crossings to thrust them back to the time of hidden caves, the dripping walls where the Mescalero Apache woman knelt and painted the male figure pointing his massive penis at the horizon, the structured dwelling where she emerged to sound the alarm—there is a rider approaching in the distance, and we don't even have a word in our language for what he is about to do.

So I entered the dust storm with my eyes opened, saw the old walls flying by, their adobe bricks spinning across the brown heavens uplifted by the terrible, summer wind. I entered the biting atmosphere of dirt, tumbleweeds, and invisible caricatures—broken hills and canyons disintegrating before my eyes, taking swift revenge on the resistance of my body as I held onto a bent cottonwood, listening to the shrieking wind pick up everything for miles and hurtle it across the desert. I cried and held on, the tears on my face turning to streaks of mud as pins of sand punctured my skin. Suddenly, the howl of the wind died down as the dust storm entered its pacifist stage—the quiet dance where the brown air is the floating world of dust, pollen, and the millions of invisible deaths swimming through the sky, covering every direction with a pure, transparent cloud whose brown curtains, brown legs, and brown shoulders embrace the living moment.

The signings of poetry are the markings of an old stone discovered falling through the torn pockets of a young boy, the decision to let it fall to the ground, a smooth pebble worn round in desert floods, shooting down the arroyos the moment the boy wanted to hear the desert rain, the second he turned around in the fragrant mud, running home with a fistful of stones he grabbed as he climbed out. This moment was the first falling sound of poetry, becoming form and theory in later, more serious times. It is bound within his large head, carried in his memory without his knowing this manner of seeing and speaking was written within the self.

I don't know what the deepest influence on my writing was—walking in fear and wonder through the deserts of El Paso or staying up late at night to make up strange little stories in notebooks I hid under the bed. One of the stories I can never forget is about a man who killed lizards and hung them on a stick he carried into the villages. He sold the dripping meat to the few people willing to eat the lizards. Not enough of them knew that lizard meat, fresh out of the desert, was one of the most nutritious and magical sources of power. The lizard man made coins from the dried meat and kept hunting lizards. He speared or knifed them in lightning quick dashes under the tumbleweeds and mesquite bushes. He was very fast and never needed a gun, each time killing a large collared lizard, then making up a poem and saying it on the spot, reciting it to himself, but never sharing it with anyone. He entered the villages with fresh lizard meat and unrecorded chants on his tongue, keeping to himself the reason why and leaving the villages after selling the meat. He had to return to his cave and be alone.

I wrote that story in one notebook I lost decades ago, before I went to high school, other journals from that time surviving in one of my locked trunks. I don't know what happened to the lizard man, though he visits every now and then. I know his unrecorded sayings can be found in the pages of my notebooks. I have known this because the villages have been eating lizard meat for generations.

In the internal world of dust, it was quiet when I rose, but no one was there to see me. They were in hiding from the flying tumbleweeds that flashed unannounced through the dirt fog, often exploding in midair like grenades, hurtling their dry thorns into the faces of the dumb and already blind. In this internal landscape of surprise, I got up from my hiding place and found the nest—the tiny lizards already breaking for the brown air, trembling and changing form as I looked down. In the internal shriek of the storm, I bent down, revising my hands, reached out for the slippery creatures, but they were already dead, the moving particles of dust announcing it was another world, another time to retrieve the bones and guess their name.

In giving in to the poem, one follows instinct based on previous patterns of memory and writing, discoveries of language and love, ways of climbing the stairs to the room not entered since childhood. This room has been kept locked for secret reasons by those who influenced the life of the poet, teaching him the words that act as tools for the workers who carried their tools into the dangerous Yaqui mines of Yuma, Arizona. The black lung in the heart of the grandfather miner is the black lung creating language within the writer, powers granted and uncontrolled by readers who insist that the secret message behind the poem is the sound they hear as they experience the poem and emerge from the mine shaft changed, yet lost.

What is the distance between this idea and the realistic invasion of having been in the mine shaft? My grandfather Bonifacio worked in those mines in 1915, cutting the stalks of germs and returning them across the valley in his lungs, before the voices echoed back to demand a different ending to the narrative sequence of poems the poet has spent four months writing. It is worth the risk, the time, the glass of milk, the puzzle on the page, the one shoe, the broken rosary, the ripe blackberry bush, the box of matches, the toad in the hole of the frog, the blank sheets of paper, and the puzzle on the page. The writer has been gone too long from this place of origins, so how can he write about it in fresh language? In his giving in to these poems and dynamiting the mine shaft of his young grandfather, the dust of each verse floats above the heavier smoke, transfixed in the drama of the poem the miner picked out of the black rock, old stones of mystery, elements and minerals of family tombs and the disintegrated molecules of reptiles devoured centuries ago—the exploding chest of lungs where the poem was embedded in the lifetime of the grandfather and in the desert stumbling of his grandson.

Last night the reoccurring dream of the rattlesnakes took place, a few days after I recited poems from my rattlesnake sequence finished several years back, stating to the audience that these regular dreams of snakes are more influential than the autobiographical details of my childhood—events worked into the poems to see if the answer to the unexpected dreams can be found. It has been several years since I have dreamed of the snakes, and I am surprised as I awaken because I left the rattlesnake sequence alone a long time ago. These dreams of crawling snakes and ground seething with rattlers that move peacefully up my legs take place after I have recited the waking moment of the snake poems in public. My stepson Charles once killed a rattler on his grandfather's ranch in Montana. He cut the tiny rattle off and gave it to me. I carried it in my backpack for a couple of years, then it disappeared from the zippered pocket. I have no idea what happened to the three-inch-long rattle, its gray cylinders a tiny instrument I could never play.

I included my rattlesnake poems in readings for years, until I got tired of sharing them. If I could find the rattle, it would bring back the story another poet friend told me about stepping on the head of a rattler during a camping trip, not seeing the sleeping thing in the grass. He didn't know it until he looked down and saw the tail whipping around his boots. He had to stand on the snake and wait until his companion ran over and killed it with a rock. The next day he was walking near a canyon stream and got too close to a huge cottonmouth snake. It raised its head and body as high as his knees, its mouth wide open, fangs glistening against the milky white throat. He ran and claims the cottonmouth almost outran him, racing after him at lightning speed until it veered suddenly and disappeared in the bushes.

My friend has tried to write a poem about being run down by a cottonmouth, but has been unable to get there. He has not dreamed about snakes like I have or written a sequence of poems about them. He is not that kind of writer, being interested in other themes. He had the rattlesnake killed so it wouldn't bite him, and the cottonmouth got tired of the chase and quit. My rattlers are not dead, and they do not chase me. They arrive in my dreams and make me write poems about returning to the hidden landscapes where they dwell, the desert thriving in natural and fenced proportions decades after I have been gone. I don't know what kind of markings or signs in the dirt the reptiles might leave behind—an alphabet that appears in the desert sand each time I wake and look, then sleep and look again. In my reoccurring dream, I don't kill snakes—letting them crawl over my body, my hair dripping with them, the earth rolling in mounds of snakes headed for a nameless river.

The chance to present a snake poem reading and snake poem workshop is tempting, an idea that gains the attention of many writers to whom I mention it, some of them admitting they have snake poems. When I read my snake poems, people react to them and tell me it is a different way to write about home, a wary approach in the hidden processes of poems where I go back to the desert without actually living there. What is this caution if I love the area and the snakes in my dreams never bite? What am I refusing to see? These are the hidden landscapes of yesterday, the paved desert roads of today, and the broken, dry canyons of tomorrow where the barbed-wire fences get closer to the snake dens in the rocks.

Audience members come up to me after my readings and tell me of their own fears and experiences with different kinds of snakes, three people sharing their dreams about the reptiles. They tell me their attempts to write about them have been frustrating. This gives me the idea for a snake poem workshop where we can talk about the meaning of snake poems and our dreams of a homeland that we can never regain or inhabit again.

The mind and energy of language and dreams fuse together behind the blue and black targets of swollen bites, inner pollen, and white fangs. In our dreams, we are consumed by memories of our past lives, then regurgitate them in poetry. In the workshop, we would also deal with our attraction to the venom and its danger—a strange impulse to dream about being bitten and finding ourselves in a different place—the hungry, painful spin where the poison gives power to the speaking old man who used to hunt lizards in the desert.

There is awareness in facing the moment of the cold thing that kept you company for years, a cold-blooded nibble of flesh and the staring slice of rattler eyes. It is the creative rattling that puts you to sleep and wakes you, dreams of origins given a chance each time a poem comes alive in the morning, each day that adds to the years of having left hidden territories behind—language of dusty arroyo, swollen Rio Grande, and torrid desert now controlled, marked off, and decorated by people who did not grow up in the Southwest of my youthful dreams. These snake eyes form around daily existence as the invisible drummer of memory and its poetic language searches among dozens of percussion and writing instruments, some hanging around his neck like cut-off rattles, his clicking and beating following you across the Sonora, the Chihuahua—the deserts of the percussive writer who must admit the hidden landscape of nonthreatening snakes is the exact spot where he was born to encounter the most lethal strike of all—the poem of the desert and the poem of home that won't leave him alone. He is the man who has been bitten numerous times and survived. His legs are black and blue diamonds as hard as the targeted veins of poisoned, swollen truth, and his poems grant him a reoccurring dream of being surrounded, escaping, then being surrounded again. The final escape comes through the first rough lines of a new poem scratched onto a notebook page when I return to El Paso, the first writing I do in my hometown in twenty years.

I wake to encounter the cold companion of desert childhood in what will become a long sequence of hissing dramas and venomous poems that never warn me before striking the page because there are two pinpricks breathing on my neck—the warning I was given when I first began to write.

About a dozen mud wasps patiently build a nest on the outside frame of the bathroom window in my mother's house. In the 100-degree heat, they work quietly, their dark wings and tiny bodies looking menacing as I stand on the other side of the screen and watch. There are no holes or torn wire in the window, so I feel secure that none of them will leave their work stations and attack me. I watch them for a long time and stare at the intricately detailed nest that is about the size and shape of a small potato, though its dull gray color and perfectly shaped tunnels remind me of the human brain. I don't know what else to compare the nest to, amazed at how this handful of wasps has created a geometric model of the universe. I get closer to the screen and wonder how long each wasp must perch there and transfer strange, life-giving liquids from its body onto the evolving form of the nest. How much building matter does each wasp carry? Do the fine chambers and delicate, paper-thin walls arise from magical juices from the wasp's internal organs, or have the wasps flown to unknown destinations and stolen microscopic materials from elsewhere? I don't know enough about wasps to answer the question. A couple of them move their wings and realign themselves on the nest. Have they noticed me spying on the magnificent job they are doing? A part of me wonders if some of them are assigned guard duty, and, if so, have they spotted me through the wire screen? Would they leave the nest to attack through the window? I forget those thoughts as I try to look into one of the tiny chambers that make up the nest.

I move a few inches closer to the screen when suddenly a hummingbird hovers a couple of feet from the window. I am startled and amazed as the hummingbird, giving off dull hues of green and gray, moves at lightning speed near the nest. For an instant, I picture the wasps going after it, but the hummingbird chirps and vanishes! In a split second, for the first time in my life, I have heard a hummingbird make a sound. This sounds ridiculous to say, but I had no idea hummingbirds could chirp like other birds. I stand there, trying to convince myself I actually saw a hummingbird fly near the wasp nest I had been observing for several minutes. Yes, it happened in an instant. In the 100-degree heat of a July in El Paso, the hummingbird brought me a good sound, adding something unimagined to my role as the witness to the silent laboring of the wasps.

The desert night lizard and the desert night snake—not the rattler, but the night snake that is always there, as if the space inside the heart is blackened with time and experience. It is dotted with stars seen only at night distance, pinpointed away from city lights that blind memory before the lights go out and I finally see that each form of darkness places great distances between the past and the present moment of blindness. I find the night stars assembling as if a strange God has given me another chance to understand how the galaxy above the landscape of home is merely the back of his hand, a wrist action sending a shooting star from southeast to northwest, its brief arrow pointing to the fingers that fall beyond those black peaks and disappear. In the desert night near Kilbourne Hole, New Mexico, there is no horizon, only the deep hole of earth shock, the volcanic formations below starting their sleep as the vast sky turns black. It does not move into a deep purple or blue, but a black that smothers thoughts of the past and signals it is time for the true world to emerge because the man standing on the edge of the ancient, extinct volcano has no idea about what is going to come out. The growing shadows consume the miles of thorny mesquite, cover the creosote bushes in a blinking of my eyes, the sudden drop of light weaving a curtain of fear and doubt about coming here to stand before a hole in the earth, wanting to find the source of its sinking scar, the scramble of black and red lava frozen in the second it takes to go from dusk to the blanket of night that filters thought upon thought, slowing things down in the caution of yucca plants that surround the invisible crater.

A man speaks in the place of stones, his arms burning night candles from the march toward home. He is talking, and his hands reach out, bells ringing in things he does not say, unable to spell what he wants, an onion he owns rolling across the table as if a planet shrunk and he could see its white ball moving beyond what he will never know. He secures the avenues from a certain wildness, says his glass eye guarded him when he was a child, saved his angels from extinction when the eye fell out one day, rolled away like the onion now tottering on the edge of the table, its axis spinning like a blind man falling because wings are not companions, only the roads to the dusty midnight floor. I suddenly look up, and huge barrel cacti are growing everywhere, sprouting like fat green bombs about to entomb the world. I do not know how to stop their growth around me. I bow my head, the swarming thorns pinning me to the ground, away from the fire I never saw, only felt at my back each night I tried to sleep on the bare desert floor.

I look across the crater as night falls and realize I will see only what the sky wants me to witness, and it is a complicated thing because I came here to find night shadows from my first visit to Kilbourne Hole, some twenty-seven years earlier when I was twenty-five and thought the black desert held the secrets to composition and creativity, the key to old speech and languages that would take me into the age of poetic imagination. I gaze across the approaching shadows and do not recognize them because I am much older and it has not taken that long to drive here from El Paso. But my hometown is gone as much as my sight has vanished because the pitch-black night suddenly covers everything around me and I am tempted to get in my car and pull the headlights on. I do not do it because I do not want to join what might be revealed in their illumination. I want to stand here and look up at the desert night and be unable to count the stars that move farther away, their immense white dots spinning in formations I can't name, can't sound or begin to describe because scientists theorize that lava flowing from nearby Aden Crater spilled over the earth's surface and cooked the wet limestone beneath me millions of years ago. After a time, there was a steam explosion that produced Kilbourne Hole, which stretches for almost two miles across and reaches a depth of nearly three hundred feet in places. It is early night and I cannot fall in. I must stand here because the shadows of youth never return when I visit the home desert. Those shapes and night patterns are gone forever. As I gaze across the desert, I recompose fear as strength, as a view that allows me temporary sight from blindness to be able to witness the night releasing a setting sun, then to wait for a light that has nothing to do with volcanic dwelling, the petrified ashes of the past sinking slowly as black time goes.

Last night I thought I heard a distant train and listened, wondering how often I had avoided crossing the tracks, the night telling me I must have been asleep. The whistle sounded far away and made me sad with the darkness of my father, the loneliness of my mother, the ghost that appeared as my grandmother who, without speaking, told me that the train was moving across the desert where her body lay. Last night I turned and stared at the window from the bed and heard the train crossing Paisano Street, weaving under Mount Cristo Rey, extending like iron smoke that won't blow away, the clacking of wheels bringing me unexpected joy before whispers announce I will never reach the train. Last night kept me from praying for what wasn't there, the diminishing whistle a guessing game, my lone chance gone after almost finding it, the whispers of old women surprising me above the silence of the quiet night train.

Flying through the night in another part of the country, wilderness was where I wanted in—geese honking overhead, vanishing in an argument of light where doubt punishes me because I can't see. It is too dark. When I said it was the desert, it was actually the road where colored lights take over and lead me into a safer sleep. Wild was not a word at the start—a shapeless form of darkness where the hawk circled, then saturated my eyes with classical light. Nothing changed but the air where I stood, the night map guiding my imagination into tomorrow's hands, the storm upon the ridge of yucca where a cold fire waited for me to rub its ashes on the rocks, leaving a message that this is the savage order of nature I was taught about by a hidden voice, the black circle in the ground an open eye that mute men leave behind in the middle of the night.

I want to leave the cut in the renamed earth behind because I can't see or find my way down the cliffs and don't want to fall into the interior, can't imagine rolling down dunes of ash to complete the voyage finally—misguided step leading me down to explore what it truly means to be aware of the desert night and its power that has followed my back for thirty years of absence from the Chihuahua Desert that hides and appears, hides and appears again, without its night resolving that there is a union of light and darkness we cannot participate in as long as we walk the welcoming landscape of a home that refuses to leave us alone.

The night's eye in the foliage of famine. The bristling coyote in the tattered cottonwoods. The graves of children burned in a fire. The change of advisors leading their souls astray. The closeness of a triangle and a tooth. The system of corn plants vanishing again, their blind roots transforming rage. The sessions from another era changing the landscape. The imitation of arrow and sharp spleen. The coat and hat left behind the adobe wall. The pebbles by the river useless and untouched. The notes of skeletal history collected to please. The night's eye in the dance of mushrooms. The speaking owl hidden in the hands. The water moving around the green logs. The stolen glance shaping all things. The flame growing on a knot in the tree. The cluster of bathed demons breathing in balance. The sudden door closed and locked. The flimsiest of reasons saving the neighborhood in the dark. The clouds moving into the distant valley at night. The phrase lying in doubt before rapture arrives. The gate to the bridge falling into the river. The game room simply a family album. The night's eye blinking for the last time. The music from the lower spheres heard too soon. The prelude about the night the moon fell.

The desert night involves knowing how to extract wisdom from action, how to move my body across the chasm and be able to get home with my eyes opened and closed, the frantic night stars moving above me as if the puzzle is being constructed across a universe that has been hidden from most of us, its mighty forces revealed about thirty miles east of El Paso in the middle of nowhere, this vast desert plain interrupted by an ancient umbilical cord cut right here, before me, as the ancient world exploded and fell into itself, surrounding hills and nearby mountains rising over time, challenging the lone rock climber to quit ascending because the desert night is about falling, not rising. The desert night is about having to totter on the edge of things in order to keep my balancing act and to be able to get into my car and manage the dirt roads back to town because night radiance is also about finding a rare, semiprecious gemstone known as peridotite or precious green olivine. This gem lies mostly on the inner eastern and northern slopes of Kilbourne above the rim rock and is found in sizes from crumbly rock to one's fist. Many collectors come here to find softball- size chunks that when broken open reveal the semiprecious olivine. Besides this green olivine, there are rusty red, gold, purple, brown, and black forms of the gem.

In the middle of the desert night, I want to bend down and grab a handful of gems from here, but I have never taken anything from the ground in decades, those younger shadows of youth having collected fossils from everywhere. Yet as I stand near my car and listen to the great silence of nothing overtaking the crater, I want to see a glistening layer of precious rocks before me and find the strength to grab them in my fist, pound them against the car door to ignite them further, watching them glow as a guide out of here. I bend to my knees near the hood of my car and recall the tarantula I spotted here twenty-seven years ago, the sudden headlights catching it as it ran under the black rocks. This time, the bristling shooting stars above me keep me from grabbing a fistful of black sand or illuminating the edge of the crater with my car. As I stated earlier, it has to be the blindness of approach, brief repose, then retreating in the night without climbing down. It is the complete movement of the night across this geologic grave that lies open to anyone who takes the time to descend. As I prepare to leave, my headlights will blaze, momentarily, and I might see what has been taken from me. Yet they will be a temporary guiding torch out of this very brief visit to an old sinking, a dry point in the desert that bridges the night with memory—a scant visit that is not made for understanding, but to think I can ward off the night and still be granted a black gift. But to receive it, I must gather the strength to open my eyes finally and adjust to a darkness that has been trying to catch up with me for years.

Renaming the world, I climb the rocks and gain a foothold before the symbols of bird and arrow, their flight barely missing me as they burn into these volcanic fields. When the Spanish crossed here, what they found on the cliffs killed them. When I reach the top of the hill, the claws of the bear slash an opening in the black crevice, the yellow paw refusing to fade for a thousand years. I pause at the top, lean on a boulder that faces the western mesas, a wing-beating thought emerging on another rock, my vision lost somewhere over the river below. I wait for others to appear, but no one ascends because the sunburst image of a face with buffalo horns waits, the edge of the cliff wide enough for one look, one leap. I keep climbing in search of the hand with missing fingers, the rock that reached into the heart of ash that erupted into formations that gave the people a place where they could carve their hands and the running deer onto walls that spoke back. I reach the highest marker, and there is nothing there, read the park sign, and turn to descend past a red vein in a smooth black rock, the red line that vanishes where the earth begins.

Acknowledgments

I thank the Rare Book Collection at the University of Texas at El Paso Library, from which much of the historical information for these essays came. I also recognize Ramon Salazar at the *El Paso Times* for his input and for giving me space in the newspaper, where some of my opinions have appeared. Support for my travels throughout the Southwest has been consistently provided by the University of Minnesota, Twin Cities, where I teach. I thank the University President's Faculty Award Committee and the Scholar of the College Fellowship Program for their recognition of my work. My family and friends in El Paso have been open in sharing their views of life on the border. This book is dedicated to them.

Sections of "A Break with the Past" appeared in the *El Paso Times*, January 18, 2004. Sections of "A Different Border" appeared in *TriQuarterly* (June 2005): 47–49; the *El Paso Times*, April 14, 2003; and *Colere* (September 2004): 11–13. Sections of "The Arches" appeared in *Many Mountains Moving* (fall 2005): 89–92 and *TriQuarterly* (June 2005): 47–49. Sections of "How to Treat People Who Have Harmed You" appeared in the *Hartnell Review* (May 2002): 9–12. "The Ladybugs" was previously published in *The New World Reader: Thinking and Writing about Global Community*, edited by Gilbert H. Muller, 189–91 (New York: Houghton Mifflin, 2005). Sections of "We Forget Who We Are" appeared in *3rd Bed* 3 (fall 2003): 14–15 and *Red Rock Review* (fall 2005): 14–17.

About the Author

Ray Gonzalez is the author of ten books of poetry, including five from BOA Editions: *The Heat of Arrivals* (1997 PEN/Oakland Josephine Miles Book Award), *Cabato Sentora* (2000 Minnesota Book Award Finalist), *The Hawk Temple at Tierra Grande* (2003 Minnesota Book Award for Poetry), *Consideration of the Guitar: New and Selected Poems* (2006 Minnesota Book Award Finalist), and *Cool Auditor* (forthcoming). *Turtle Pictures* (University of Arizona Press, 2000), a mixed-genre text, received the 2001 Minnesota Book Award for Poetry. His poems have appeared in the 1999, 2000, and 2003 editions of *The Best American Poetry* and *The Pushcart Prize: Best of the Small Presses* 2000. He is also the author of a collection of essays, *The Underground Heart: A Return to a Hidden Landscape* (University of Arizona Press, 2002), which received the 2003 Carr P. Collins/Texas Institute of Letters Award for Best Book of Non-fiction; was named one of ten best Southwest books of the year by the Arizona Humanities Commission and one of the best nonfiction books of the year by the *Rocky Mountain News*; was a Minnesota Book Award Finalist in Memoir; and was selected as a book of the month by the El Paso Public Library. Another nonfiction book, *Memory Fever* (University of Arizona Press, 1999), is a memoir about growing up in the Southwest. Gonzalez has written two collections of short stories, *The Ghost of John Wayne* (University of Arizona Press, 2001), winner of a 2002 Western Heritage Award for Best Short Story and a 2002 Latino Heritage Award in Literature, and *Circling the Tortilla Dragon* (2002). His second mixed-genre text, *The Religion of Hands* (volume 2 of the Turtle Pictures trilogy) was published by the University of Arizona Press in 2005 and received a 2006 Latino Heritage Best Book of Poetry Award. He is the editor of twelve anthologies, most recently *No Boundaries: Prose Poems by 24 American Poets* (2002). Gonzalez has served as poetry editor of the *Bloomsbury Review* for twenty-five years and founded

LUNA, a poetry journal, in 1998. He received a 2004 Lifetime Achievement Award in Literature from the Border Regional Library Association. He is a full professor in the MFA Creative Writing Program at the University of Minnesota in Minneapolis.

Library of Congress Cataloging-in-Publication Data

González, Ray.
  Renaming the earth : personal essays / Ray Gonzalez.
     p.   cm. (Camino del sol)
   ISBN 978-0-8165-2410-5 (alk. paper) —
   ISBN 978-0-8165-2407-5 (pbk. : alk. paper)
   1. González, Ray—Homes and haunts—Mexican-
American Border Region.   2. Mexican Americans—
Mexican-American Border Region—Social conditions.
3. Mexican-American Border Region—Social conditions.
4. Human ecology—Mexican-American Border Region.
I. Title.
PS3557.O476Z46   2008
814'.54—dc22   2008022510